Microsoft Dataverse

MICROSOFT DATAVERSE
THE POWER PLATFORM SERIES

DAVID YACK

Leveraging Microsoft Dataverse to build real world business solutions.

Microsoft Dataverse

Published by

We Speak You Learn, LLC
430 Beacon Lite #135
Monument CO 80132

https://365.Training

Copyright 2021 by We Speak You Learn, LLC and David Yack

Limit of Liability/Disclaimer of Warranty: The author and publisher have taken care in the preparation of this book, but make no expressed or implied warranty of any kind and assume no responsibility for errors or omissions. No liability is assumed for incidental or consequential damages in connection with or arising out of the use of the information or programs contained herein. The advice and strategies contained herein may not be suitable for every situation. This work is sold with the understanding that the publisher is not engaged in rendering legal, accounting, or other professional services. If professional assistance is required, the services of a competent professional person should be sought. Neither the publisher nor the author shall be liable for damages arising herefrom. The fact that an organization or Website is referred to in this work as a citation and/or a potential source of further information does not mean that the author or the publisher endorses the information the organization or Website may provide or recommendations it may make. Further, readers should be aware that Internet Websites listed in this work may have changed or no longer exist between when this work was written and when it is read.

All rights reserved. No part of this publication may be reproduced, stored in a retrieval system, or transmitted, in any form or by any means, electronic, mechanical, photocopying, recording, or otherwise, without the prior written consent of the publisher. Printed in the United States of America.

About the Author

David Yack is the CTO of Colorado Technology Consultants, based in Colorado. He is recognized by Microsoft as a Regional Director and a Business Applications MVP. As a senior hands on technology and business consultant with over 20 years of industry experience, David enjoys developing applications on the Microsoft platforms, specializing in large system architecture and design. David helps clients migrate and build new applications on the technology, as well as helping to mentor and train their staffs.

David's current focus is on the ***Microsoft Power Platform, Dynamics 365 and Azure*** *cloud solutions.* David is a Microsoft Certified Professional and a Microsoft Certified Trainer. As a trainer, David has delivered trainings globally to both developers and functional consultants.

As an author, David has been involved in multiple books on .NET and Business Application topics. David has also published virtual training courses on Pluralsight, 365.Training, Microsoft Learn and Microsoft edX

David is a frequent speaker at user group and industry events He lives in Colorado with his wife and three dogs. You can always track David down via his blog at http://blog.davidyack.com

Credits

Editor: Julie Yack

Book Designer: Julie Yack

Acknowledgments

A special thanks to my wife Julie who is always supportive of me when I tell her I am writing another book. You can thank her eagle eye for fixing typos as well as her expert understanding of the topic for greatly improving the quality of what you are reading today.

I'd also like to thank the following people who took the time to review and provide feedback on the early drafts of the content. I'm pretty sure when they volunteered, they thought it was only a few pages to review ☺ Check out the links next to their names to see the great stuff they are producing.

George Doubinski - https://doubin.ski/

Joel Lindstrom - https://crm.audio/

James Novak - https://futurezconsulting.com/blog/

Mark Smith - https://www.nz365guy.com/

Jerry Weinstock - https://www.crminnovation.com/blog/

Matt Wittemann - https://mattwittemann.com/

Natraj Yegnaraman - https://dreamingincrm.com/

Nick Doelman - https://readyxrm.blog/

Introduction

As businesses look to modernize their line of business applications Microsoft Power Platform is the tool of choice to accelerate and implement digital transformation. Microsoft Power Platform is made up of Power Apps, Power Automate, Power BI and Power Virtual Agent.

Microsoft Dataverse is a key component of the Power Platform and provides for data storage and related business logic execution. Dataverse implements Microsoft's Common Data Model (CDM) allowing it to be part of the data fabric in an organization with a common way of describing core business data.

In this book, we are focused on using Microsoft Dataverse to build business applications. Specifically, we will look at the capabilities required to build data models for real world business applications. These applications can be built by power users (e.g. Joe or Sue from accounting) or by professional app makers whose job is focused on building Power Platform solutions.

Differences between this and Microsoft Docs

This book on Microsoft Dataverse is intended to supplement the Microsoft documentation. Microsoft, on the docs site, will typically provide a detailed reference of all the details related to the platform. This book does not attempt to provide that level of reference detail and in many cases will defer to the docs site. The docs site will also provide a very broad guide and samples for the platform in this case there may be some overlap in what we cover, but typically the samples will be different, and we will go into more details and provide a consultant's perspective. What do we mean by a consultant's perspective? When writing documentation for a product you must be 100% complete and provide guidance that is broadly relevant to the majority of users. In this book we are focused on real word implementations and we will attempt to give the consultant's perspective and ways to look for creative solutions.

Who is this book for?

The target audience for this book is solution architects and app makers that are building applications inside their companies. It is also for those packaging up to resell as part of an ISV solution deployed on the Power Platform. Finally, it is for the consultant who is the road warrior helping companies customize the platform for their business needs. In fact, anyone building solutions that will help automate and manage internal business processes can benefit from its insight.

Contents overview

Chapter 1-Microsoft Dataverse Overview – What is Microsoft Dataverse and when to use it as part of your data and business logic strategy. This includes understanding the core capabilities, architecture and high-level licensing.

Chapter 2- Common Data Model Overview – Understand how the Microsoft Common Data model is used by Dataverse and how you should leverage it when building your Dataverse data model.

Chapter 3- Tables – **Tables** are the key building block for storing data in Dataverse. Learn about the different types of tables, ownership and how to decide between custom and Common Data Model entity definitions.

Chapter 4- Working with columns – Each Dataverse table is a collection of columns that store the individual data elements. Each column has a data type. Learn about all the different Dataverse data types and how to choose the best one for your data.

Chapter 5- Relationships – Relationships bring real world data models to life by describing the connections between business data (tables). This chapter explores how to use relationships and to select the right relationship behaviors based on your data and business requirements.

Chapter 6- Data Modeling – At the heart of any good line of business application is the data model. Dataverse allows app builders to declaratively build the data model and work with it using all the power of the platform. This chapter is a must-read for a good understanding of the decisions made when data modeling.

Chapter 7- Security Modeling – Just as important as the data model, in this chapter we look at security modeling. Here we cover all the security building blocks Microsoft Dataverse provides and then review considerations for building a good model.

Data Modeling Scenarios – There is no one size fits all for data modeling so one of the best ways to learn about it is via scenarios. Join us at https://365l.ink/Dataverse - Click Enroll now you will be asked to provide a few words from the chapters of the book and then you will get free access to the additional content. Give us your ideas there on what scenarios are challenging you and look for us to keep adding more content there.

Where do I get more?

Your learning doesn't have to stop with the pages of this book but can continue on to our website https://365.training. In fact, use the direct link of https://365l.ink/Dataverse - Click Enroll now you will be asked to provide a few words from the chapters of the book and then you will get free access to the content.

What Software Do I Need?

In order to develop using the ideas and techniques presented in this book you will need access to a Microsoft Dataverse environment. The simplest way to obtain that is to sign up for a community plan license. You can find details of that here https://powerapps.microsoft.com/en-us/communityplan/

What about stuff we screwed up…You know Errata

In the process of writing, everyone sure wanted to make sure it was 100% accurate, but since nobody is perfect, we are sure you might find a few typos or other things that aren't correct. We would love to hear your feedback and will do our best to incorporate it into the next printing of the book. You can look at our website, https://365l.ink/Dataverse for any last-minute changes. Feel free to email us as well, info@365.training if you find a typo.

1

Microsoft Dataverse Overview

The Microsoft Dataverse is a cloud service that provides data storage, security, and data layer business logic execution for line of business apps. Dataverse is designed to make it easy to build business applications as part of the Power Platform. Power Apps, Power Automate, Power BI, and Power Virtual Agents are the key components of the Power Platform and all have first class support for working with data stored in Dataverse. We will explore that throughout the rest of the content.

Dataverse stores data organized into tables which have sets of rows. Dataverse tables are different from directly storing in a typical database table or equivalent because they provide an abstraction on top of those adding additional value we will explore throughout the content. What do we mean by abstraction? In addition to tables full of related data, you get the full power of the platform that includes features like a security layer to define access to data; automation to provide ease of use and reduction of repetitive tasks; a fast way to expose the data to users through model-driven apps; an API for professional developers; and more. Each table has columns that store the individual data elements. The Common Data Model (CDM) defines some core entities that every Dataverse environment starts with and then you can create your own custom tables and columns to support your specific business scenarios, as well as customizing the standard elements from the CDM in your Dataverse database.

Microsoft Dataverse

Note: Previously, Dataverse tables were named entities and you will likely encounter usage of both entity and table to describe them. Also, columns were also called fields and attributes. In fact, for developers using the APIs they will keep using the old terminology when using the API messages.

It's important to understand that the Common Data Model (CDM) is just the specification of entities and attributes, it's often called the schema. CDM itself is not an implementation, think of it more like a reusable data model design. CDM is a way for Microsoft to establish a common set of definitions that can be reused. While Dataverse implements the Common Data Model core set of entities as tables in every environment, Dataverse is not the only implementor of the CDM. CDM can be implemented in any application in any data store. We will explore more on the CDM in the second module.

The following diagram visually shows how Dataverse fits in with the overall Power Platform.

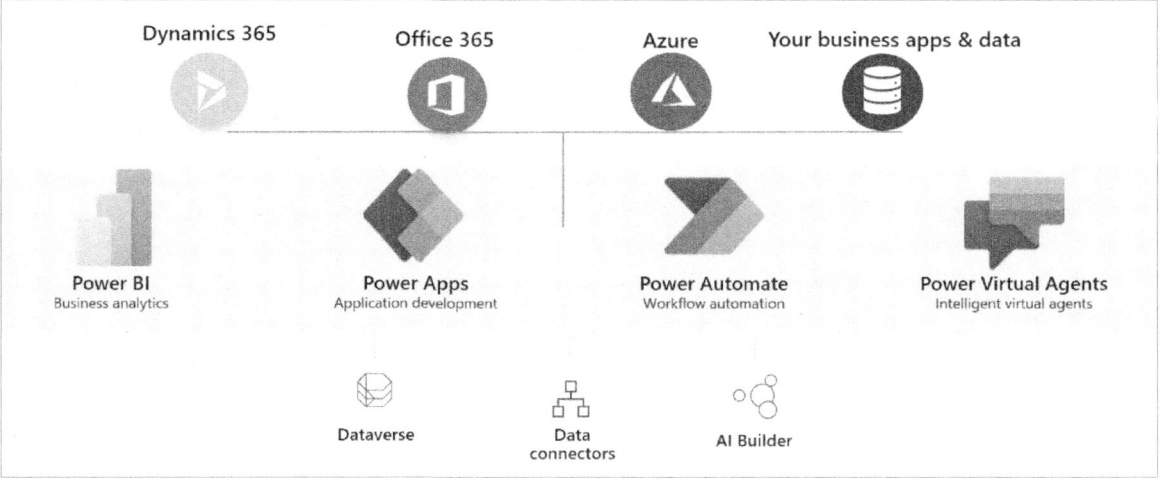

Dataverse is an abstraction on top of Microsoft's core data technologies. This abstraction makes Dataverse a hybrid data storage service because it uses multiple techniques to store its data. Common data types like text columns and numbers are stored in Azure SQL while files and photos are stored in common blob storage. And yet other types of data such as telemetry are stored in more document-centric storage. All this data type specific storage however is hidden from the app builder and handled by the platform to optimize how applications are built and run. This abstraction also lets your app benefit from the best of Microsoft data storage technologies. That would include being able to adopt new enhancements without impacting your application. Dataverse also manages compute resources allowing in-platform execution of custom business logic at the data layer. This includes declarative business rules that don't require code development and deeper developer code extensibility via plug-ins. Dataverse also offers extensibility with Azure functions and other external systems through published events. This allows processing to be handed off for processing.

Most people never have to worry about how Dataverse works internally and that is by design. The abstractions ensure that Microsoft has the flexibility to evolve the internals to take advantage of new capabilities without impacting the applications you build as directly.

For those curious of what goes on inside of Dataverse, the following diagram is a good high-level illustration of Dataverse's internal architecture.

For those that don't want that level of detail that is ok too, you don't need to be aware of how things work inside Dataverse. Just know that Dataverse is designed to take advantage of Microsoft's Cloud enhancements and make it as transparent as possible for you to evolve your application on Dataverse.

The history of Dataverse

While the name Microsoft Dataverse is new, the core engine for Dataverse came from Dynamics 365 (and before that Microsoft Dynamics CRM). The core technology has evolved from an on-premise only data engine to the cloud scale service it is today. In fact, if you are running a Dynamics 365 customer engagement app (Sales, Customer Service, Field Service, Marketing) in your company that data is stored in Dataverse. This evolution demonstrates the ability of the architecture to evolve. During this evolution applications built with supported customization techniques were able to also evolve with minimal impact.

To arrive at the Microsoft Dataverse, Microsoft essentially gave a name to the underlying data engine and separated it from the customer engagement apps (Sales, Service, Field Service and Marketing). This allows today for Dataverse to be used by Microsoft apps as well as your own custom apps all in the same Dataverse environment, with or without dependencies on one another. Prior to being named Dataverse it was also named the Common Data Service. You will likely still see many references to Dataverse still using that older name.

The following are some names or terminology you might encounter and how they fit in with the modern-day Microsoft Dataverse.

CRM	Customer Relationship Management – but often used as a reference to the equivalent of Dataverse. For example, "I need to add a field to the CRM database" essentially is adding a column to a Dataverse table.
XRM	XRM is a play on CRM, where C means customer, X means anything. It was a popular way to refer to the product in a generic way to get people to understand they could build more than just CRM solutions. People still use this term today to refer to Dataverse, and in Dataverse you will still find this used in the naming of developer tools and APIs.
CDS	CDS is short for Common Data Service and now represents Microsoft Dataverse.

Microsoft Dataverse for Teams

At the same time Microsoft renamed the Common Data Service to Microsoft Dataverse they also introduced Microsoft Dataverse for Teams. While it is easy to think that means simply using Microsoft Dataverse from within Microsoft Teams it really represents much more. Microsoft Dataverse for Teams is really a subset of the overall Power Platform available for use within the Team's client. Anyone that is licensed for Microsoft Teams can build and use apps, automation and chatbots that run within the Teams client. This makes Microsoft Dataverse for Teams a low-code data platform built-in to Teams. This is good news because it makes Microsoft Dataverse available to a much bigger audience with simplified licensing.

Now you are probably wanting to know more about the difference between Microsoft Dataverse and Microsoft Dataverse for Teams? The easiest way to think about this is think of Microsoft Dataverse for Teams as being a licensing package that includes the ability to use best of the Power Platform tools needed to build apps, automations and chatbots. This also includes a subset of the overall Microsoft Dataverse capabilities. Some people refer to this as Microsoft Dataverse lite.

The subset of Microsoft Dataverse includes all the things needed to build apps in the context of Microsoft Teams. When enabled in a team, a Power Platform environment with Microsoft Dataverse is associated with that team. This environment has the same core capabilities as when Microsoft Dataverse is used standalone. The following are the most significant differences:

- **Storage capacity** – Each environment supports up to 2 GB per team which supports up to 1 million rows. To grow beyond you would upgrade to the full Microsoft Dataverse which can handle 4 TB or more.

- **Data types** – Only basic data types are included. Advanced data types like multi-currencies require upgrade.

- **Developer API** – Developer API access and building plug-in extensions is not available. Using Power Automate with the Microsoft Dataverse connector can handle many of the scenarios where this would be required.

- **Simplified security** - Microsoft Dataverse security is simplified and focused on the team members and guests. Advanced security constructs like field level security, hierarchical security, record sharing is not available without upgrading.

You can drill into more detail in a feature-by-feature comparison here Dataverse for Teams vs. Dataverse - Power Apps | Microsoft Docs

The good news is the core knowledge and skills you'll learn as part of this content apply to both.

Microsoft Dataverse

Microsoft Dataverse for Teams is targeted at true citizen developers. So, while as a full-on app maker you may see this as a set of limitations, to a citizen app maker this is all new functionality that opens them to a world of app making that wasn't available before.

For a more detailed introduction to Dataverse for Teams, you can try out this course from 365.Training Introducing Microsoft Dataverse for Teams | 365.Training

What are environments?

In the Power Platform, when you build Power Apps or Power Automate flows these are all built in the context of an environment. Think of environments as a resource container tracking all the resources you build. Environments are tied to a geographic region, and default to your Azure Active Directory tenant location. Currently to change an environment's geographic region, you must submit a support request.

A tenant can have multiple environments. For example, they might have them for different business lines or they can be used to separate development, testing and live production resources.

Dataverse is provisioned in the context of an environment. Each environment can have a single Dataverse instance associated. When you provision Dataverse in an environment you configure the base currency and language, this base language and base currency cannot be changed once configured. You can add additional languages and currencies.

A key thing to know about environments with Dataverse is that each has their own table and column definitions as well as their own business data. To transport the same definitions to other environments solutions are used as containers to copy the customizations.

What are Solutions?

Solutions are containers used to track a group of customizations you make. This includes tables, their columns and any other assets including Power Apps and Power Automate flows. An environment can have multiple solutions. Solutions can depend on other solutions, where the set of solutions together represent the entire business application.

Solutions can be exported and imported into other environments that have Dataverse provisioned. For ISVs (Independent Software Vendors), solutions are packaged as a deployment package and published on AppSource. When someone does an installation of one of the AppSource listings one or more solution files will be imported (installed) in your environment, similar to how you might manually do the import yourself.

As you start a new project, the best thing to do is to create a solution that will hold all the customizations related to that project. For example, if I was creating an event management app, I would create a solution named Dave's Event Management. Associated with that solution is what is referred to as a publisher. The publisher in my example might be the company name Dave, LLC and, to more easily identify the components of my solution and prevent naming collisions, I would specify a customization prefix of "dave". That prefix is used as the first part of the name of any tables, columns, apps and other resource you define as part of that solution. For example, if you created an Event table, the actual unique name for that table would be dave_event.

Note: *Even if you don't create your own solution, each environment with Dataverse enabled comes with a solution named either Common Data Service Default Solution or Microsoft Dataverse Default Solution and the assets you create (like tables and columns) are tracked there. This is fine for personal productivity apps, but for planned apps it's best to create your own custom solution just for that planned app.*

Dynamics 365 and Dataverse

Surprisingly one of the more common questions I get is something like "I have Dynamics 365 for Sales, can I use Dataverse?". And my answer is also surprisingly simple, you already do use Dataverse. When you sign up for Dynamics 365 customer engagement applications (Sales, Service, Field Service, etc.) they all get an environment with Dataverse provisioned. In that Dataverse the Dynamics 365 app solutions are installed. This provisions more than just the core CDM entities but also the CRM related parts of the Common Data Model.

The other similar question I get is related to Dynamics 365 Finance and Operations, Dynamics 365 Business Central and Dynamics 365 GP. For these questions I have some sad news. While these all share the Dynamics 365 brand, each have their own unique data store that is not Dataverse. There is an integration service built-in to Dataverse that provides scenario-based integration between Dataverse and Dynamics 365 Finance and Operations. An example of this would be to synchronize the data for a prospect to cash scenario where data goes between Sales and Finance to complete the process from prospect to cash. Additionally, Microsoft also has dual write technology for core tables involving customer data. Dual write would keep the data in sync automatically between the two data stores.

More than just a table

It's easy to just think of Dataverse like any other data repository and all you get is a place to store some data. When you create a table in Dataverse you get several features that in most data stores would require you to build custom code.

- **Security model** – Security is a core concept of Dataverse with each table you create being automatically included as part of its role-based security features.

- **Forms** – Forms can be used by Power Apps to present the details of a table row to the user. Default forms are created when you create new tables, and these can be customized. You can create custom forms as well.

- **Views** – Views can be used by Power Apps to present a list of table rows to the user. View criteria filters the total available rows to a subset matching the criteria.

- **Process automation and guidance** – Each table created can automatically trigger automation to run upon common events like create, update and delete. Business process flows can be created to guide users through the stages of the process and can be created across multiple tables to make the user experience better, so they do not have to understand the underlying data model.

- **Business rules and code logic** – Business rules can be created to enforce common business requirements such as dynamic data requirements and validation. For more complex scenarios developers can use code to hook into the platform operations such as saving data to have their code extensions run as if the code was built into the platform.

- **Developer API** – A common task for business applications is for developers to create an API to allow access to the data. Dataverse automatically creates a RESTful API that uses the OData V4 protocol for working with the table data and services. All interactions with the API enforce the business rules and logic that have been configured for the table along with enforcing the security model.

- **Power Apps user features** – Power Apps users automatically get features like import/export of data, integration with Excel, personalization features to create views and dashboards as well as many features such as recently used records that just light up in the app without any custom code being required. Some of these features can be limited by using the role-based security mentioned above.

- **Building apps** – Power Apps makes it easy to build apps that use Dataverse data. From the Power Apps studio, you can easily add columns to Dataverse that are missing. Power Apps makes it easy to use Dataverse relationships to navigate data presented to the user in an app.

In total, new Dataverse tables create a foundation of features that benefit app builders to reduce the amount of customization they need to create.

Comparing Dataverse to other data storage technologies

You have a wide variety of choices for where you store your business application data. Dataverse will always enjoy the best support within the Power Platform. In this section, we'll review some considerations for evaluating common alternatives you might be considering.

- **Microsoft Excel** – Often the starting point for the automation of many business applications because it is broadly used by business users. Excel is good for mostly static data that doesn't have complex data relationships. Excel's equivalent of a table would be a worksheet. Excel lacks enterprise scale and manageability, making it not appropriate for anything but the smallest uses. Dataverse provide the ability to import from Excel allowing a good path for migration of apps that started with this as a data source.

- **Microsoft Access** – Microsoft Access has been a staple in starter business apps because it came with the Microsoft Office licenses. Apps built on Microsoft Access were classically forms over data with any logic being specific to that one app. However, Dataverse can have logic at the data layer that is used by multiple apps without requiring re-implementation. Power Apps built on Dataverse also have a large eco system of connectors to include other services' data without having to do complex integration. Like Excel, Microsoft Access lacks the robust security model capabilities and scale for enterprise deployments. Power Apps also let the user choose what device or browser they want to use and require a minimal footprint on the device as they are cloud-based applications. Many Access apps have been around for years and are good candidates for updating to the Power Platform. You can now easily migrate Access data to Dataverse.

- **Microsoft SharePoint** – Many Power Apps get their start with using stored data in SharePoint lists. SharePoint is attractive from a licensing point of view because it is included as part of Microsoft Office 365 licenses that users already have. The rush to use something that doesn't have additional costs can prevent proper evaluation of the business value Dataverse might offer. For simple data with simplistic security requirements SharePoint lists are more than adequate. SharePoint started out focused on collaboration and added more app data storage features as it evolved. Dataverse on the other hand started out focused on app data management and building apps quickly on that data. Key things like ability to have assigned owners and complex record and column security as well as deep integration with business logic can often make Dataverse an easy choice over SharePoint. SharePoint is not as strong as Dataverse as you start needing to relate data across multiple lists and try to compose a full data model. From an app building standpoint, much of the working with data and relationship via Power Apps and Power Automate is easier and more powerful on Dataverse than it is on SharePoint lists. Consider a SharePoint list similar to a table in Dataverse. SharePoint app makers should consider Dataverse if their app involves beyond more than a list or two. Dataverse should also be considered anytime there is any amount of business rules or logic that needs to be consistently implemented across the data. Dataverse also has good support for localization and multi-currency scenarios. Having a full application lifecycle of dev, test, and production works better with Dataverse because it is packaged and transported between environments as a solution. Similar SharePoint apps require multiple deployment packages to accomplish the same promotion from dev, to test to production.

- **SQL Server** – Unlike Excel or Access, applications built on SQL Server scale and are designed for enterprise use. Using SQL Server however lacks many of the abstractions that Dataverse offers, meaning that the building of constructs like data security are pushed onto the app builder. Most business app builders would find similar capabilities in Dataverse over SQL Server with the exception being high volume applications. If you are building a stock trading platform with billions of daily API requests there are clear advantages to not having the Dataverse abstraction layer, but for most line of business applications the overhead of the abstractions is of minimal impact and outweighed by the benefits it provides. One of the most commonly noticed design implications of moving something from direct SQL Server to Dataverse is around normalization. Typical relational data models are very normalized where Dataverse data models can be less normalized to ensure the best user experience and to simplify building of the apps. Because of the abstractions, building apps can be easier for less technical app builders than apps built directly on SQL Server.

- **Non-Microsoft technologies** – While the above list focuses on Microsoft technologies you can apply much of the same reasoning to evaluate non-Microsoft technologies.

An important thing to remember about building apps on the Power Platform is you don't HAVE to move data into Dataverse to benefit from the platform, however doing so will give you a great data platform to quickly build applications. Understanding this opens other scenarios that aren't pure Dataverse but use Dataverse as part of an overall solution.

Earlier I mentioned that Dataverse isn't ideal for super high-volume transaction systems like a stock trading platform. That includes apps that have a high volume of bulk updates (e.g. you're updating hundreds of millions of records daily). Now that doesn't mean you can't use Dataverse as part of the solution, it just means you might focus on storing the data with high volume directly in Azure SQL or another high-volume data storage engine, and store data like the customer or related low volume data in Dataverse. Power Apps can surface data from both data sources into a single app which will hide the fact it uses two data stores from the users. Of course, the parts of the app that use Dataverse will be easier to compose the app as the tooling continues to include more first class Dataverse app building experiences.

As an example, our 365.Training website (https://365.training) uses a different approach. All the data is stored in Dataverse, but the website doesn't always pull data from Dataverse throughout the day. Instead, data from Dataverse is brought into Azure Cosmos DB and the website pulls from that as needed. The data in Azure Cosmos is stored in documents optimized for use by the website. Rather than requiring 75-100 queries to present a page, one document has all the data required. Azure Cosmos DB has the ability to replicate data in multiple geographies providing the quickest access to instances of the web site in different regions. Now if we had built the app to maintain all the metadata of the training content directly on Azure Cosmos DB, it would have taken many hours more to build the app. Instead, by having the data originate in Dataverse, we use a Power Apps model-driven app for the primary management of the data, and it was built in a minimal amount of time. The key point here is that data can originate and be managed in Dataverse but can be moved elsewhere to facilitate optimal processing as needed.

As you think of how to use Dataverse as part of your app don't be afraid to get creative and mix it with either existing storage or with other modern data storage techniques to best meet your app requirements.

Building Apps on Dataverse data

It's likely you got here because you were already building Power Apps and just not using Dataverse. However, in case you aren't familiar let's talk for a minute about building apps using Dataverse data. The most logical choice for building apps is using Power Apps. Power Apps offers a low code approach to building apps where you use formulas or configuration to compose the application structure and logic. Power Apps offers two types of applications to start from, canvas and model-driven. Canvas leverages connectors as the data source and is great for working with all kinds of data. Model-driven is only available when Dataverse is provisioned. Model-driven gets its name by being tied to the data model you define in Dataverse. Essentially it is the quickest way to build a forms over data application on the Power Platform. Model-driven apps are usable via web or mobile devices and offer built-in responsive design to the device or browser size without any additional effort by the app maker.

Power Apps Portals offer another way to build applications on top of Dataverse data – these are more like a traditional web application that can be used to reach both internal and external users.

With the introduction of Microsoft Dataverse for Teams you can now also start the app building process from the Microsoft Teams client. A simplified visual editor is available to define the data model and populate data.

Of course, you can still use all the custom development techniques from Xamarin to your favorite JavaScript developer library to build an application that acts as a front-end for Dataverse data. However, you should always look first at what Power Apps offers before you go completely custom. A strong benefit of Power Apps is the low maintenance, multi-language, and accessible capabilities of the apps that can often be expensive to reproduce. This custom approach is best reserved for external customer facing mobile apps where a truly custom experience can be a competitive differentiation. For internal and partner facing apps, looking to Power Apps and using some custom Power Apps Component Framework (PCF) controls is the best approach. PCF allows taking over the rendering for a column or part of the content on a screen/form to include a completely custom experience.

Whichever app approach you take, know that Power Apps will always have Dataverse tooling that optimizes for building apps that take advantage of Dataverse data.

Getting data into Dataverse

There are multiple ways to get data into Dataverse. Microsoft provides built-in tools and also 3rd parties offer solutions for more complex requirements. The most common scenarios for doing this are either initial data loading into Dataverse or in support of ongoing integrations.

The provided import tools are good for simple scenarios and low volumes of data. There are two primary options for working with data. First, one that works with Excel and CSV files. This approach provides basic mapping of data from the import into Dataverse.

The other option, Data flows leverages Power Query for data transformation. This opens import data sources to a larger set of providers including SQL Server, Salesforce, OData feeds, Web APIs and more. From these data sources Power Query provides the ability to do transforms like splitting columns and more advanced data mapping. If you have used Power Query for other data transformation tasks you will already be familiar with how to use the import transformation capabilities.

As your volume and complexity increases tools like Kingswaysoft's adapter for Microsoft SQL Server Integration Services offer a lot of configurability as well as ability to handle higher volumes. These tools also offer the familiar capabilities of SSIS for orchestrating the import process and often companies already have resources familiar and the only thing they are learning are the Dataverse specific aspects of the Dataverse data source. I would look to these tools as your volume of data exceeds 100,000 records or you have more complex pre-processing you need to do.

Pro tip: *Staging data in an Azure virtual machine and running integration tools like Scribe or Kingswaysoft from there instead of your local network will often drastically improve the performance of your data integration processing.*

For moving reference data like a list of categories and other more static data that might need to exist in multiple environments with Dataverse you can use the Configuration Migration Tool. This tool allows data to be exported and re-imported and includes logic for updating existing records in the target environments.

For ongoing integrations, Power Automate or Azure Logic Apps with the Dataverse connectors can facilitate collecting data from the outside world and storing it in Dataverse.

Getting data out of Dataverse

Users with appropriate security privileges can export data to Excel using the built-in capabilities. Any tool designed to connect to an OData Web API and also supporting Azure AD authentication can be used with Dataverse data.

Similar to how we discussed 3rd party connectors for getting data into Dataverse, most of those same ISVs provide support for querying and extracting subsets of data from Dataverse. Common scenarios here include bringing data out for building data warehouses or other analytics solutions.

Power Automate and Azure Logic apps can be scheduled to prepare data to be sent to external systems and using connectors or direct APIs of the external systems to publish data to complete automated integrations.

Dataverse can also be configured to export data to Azure SQL or Azure Data Lake/Azure Synapseon a recurring basis. This supports scenarios where you need to do bulk processing and you don't want to burden the operational Dataverse data store with the load.

Another capability of Dataverse is to publish events that occur in Dataverse out to external systems for further processing and integration. Any create, update, delete or custom action that occurs in Dataverse can be pushed externally to Azure Service Bus, Azure Event Hub or to any listener that supports a webhook registration. This event publishing capability makes Dataverse a candidate to consider for maintaining data centrally, and then using the events to notify other systems of changes.

Securing Dataverse data

When you provision Dataverse in an environment, Dataverse security roles take over control of security and the environment only roles are mapped to Dataverse roles. Dataverse security roles are a set of privileges with associated access levels that are configurable for each resource. Users can be assigned security roles directly or can gain them through their association with a Dataverse team. Dataverse teams can have their members dynamically managed by associating it with an Azure AD group.

Through these associations, users can acquire privileges from multiple security roles. An important concept to understand is that when this happens the user's actual access is accumulated across the multiple roles with the greatest level of access prevailing. For example, if one role provides the user with no read access to the Account table and another provides the same user with full organization level access, then the user will have full access. Once you give a user access to a privilege, another role can't reduce that privilege.

Microsoft Dataverse

The security constructs of Dataverse are applied to all apps that are built to use the Dataverse data. This ensures the core security requirements you design are consistently implemented across apps and not dependent on the app builder. This means regardless what type of Power App or Power Automate flow you build security is consistently enforced.

Another key concept to understand is that each table you create starts with zero user access. Part of properly configuring Dataverse and a new table is configuring a security role giving users proper access to the data. There is one security role that has automatic organization wide access to every table and that is the System Administrator. When Dataverse is provisioned the environment owner is automatically assigned the System Administrator role.

Licensing Dataverse

The most common way of licensing Dataverse is either via the Power Apps license or one of the Dynamic 365 app licenses. Both of these include storage entitlements for Dataverse which is effectively how Dataverse is licensed. In the past, Dataverse used to be licensed by the environment and the number of environments was limited to specific numbers by license types. Current licensing is based on storage size. This allows you to have as many environments as you want with Dataverse as long as you have at least 1GB of available storage. In addition to getting more storage for each licensed user, you can also directly purchase additional storage. You can now also Pay-as-you-go using an Azure subscription.

With the introduction of Microsoft Dataverse for Teams a new simplified licensing model is available because it is bundled with Microsoft Teams. For applications that require collaboration with a large number of internal people or business guests this can be a good fit for many scenarios.

How to customize Dataverse

There are three ways to customize Dataverse. The following are the supported ways to make and manage customizations in an environment that has Dataverse provisioned.

Technique	Description
Web Editor	Using the Power Apps maker portal at https://make.powerapps.com you can customize Dataverse including creating tables, columns and relationships. This method is typically used to establish the initial data model and for ongoing maintenance. This can be done by any user that has been given the customization security role or is an environmental admin.

Import/Export	Most of the customizations can be exported to a compressed zip file that contains an xml file using the export solution feature. This produces a file of the components in the solution that can be later be imported into another environment that has Dataverse. This is often used to move changes between a development and a test/ production type environment.
Web API	Dataverse also has the ability to let developers use the Web API to manipulate the metadata in addition to simply being able to query it. This technique is typically targeted to ISVs that will be installing their solution repeatedly. Unlike the import technique, the Web API can be used to automate the removal of items from the data model.

Community Tools

In addition to the tools provided by Microsoft, the external community has come together to build some useful tools to make building apps on Dataverse more productive.

- **XrmToolBox** – This is a large collection of tools that all run within the context of a hosting application called XrmToolBox. This is a downloaded app that runs locally and connects to Dataverse. You can find more details here - https://www.xrmtoolbox.com/

- **CDS.Tools** - This is an online site that has a collection of tools that work with Dataverse. These tools run in the cloud and don't require any local installation. You can learn more at https://CDS.Tools

MVP tips for getting started with Dataverse

I asked some of the other business application MVPs for their top tips to get started with Dataverse and here is what they suggested:

- Think point and click first. Then if necessary, code. – Jerry Weinstock
- Don't think like a developer. Think about security early and don't wait until the end to lock things down. – Jim Novak
- Think of Dataverse as Microsoft Access in the cloud…but better. All the goodness of Access without the limitations. – Nick Doelman

- Don't get stuck thinking information model first all the time. Think usability and processes and let the model evolve. – Jonas Rapp
- Think about what reports/analytics/insights you need and don't wait until testing to think about the data you need to capture for outcomes. – Mike Ochs
- Think of Dataverse as not just a database, but a platform with a database, multiple languages and currencies, granular security, and integration with other Microsoft platforms. It handles the plumbing of your business applications, letting you focus on delivering a great user experience. – Joel Lindstrom
- Users don't care how we organize data as long as we present it to them in an easy to consume experience. – Julie Yack

Wrapping it up

One of the most flexible concepts the Power Platform provides is the ability to access your data where it already exists using connectors. Dataverse however provides for first class data storage of business app data. Dataverse should be your first consideration if you don't already have an existing data store due to its tight integration with Power Apps, Power Automate, Power Virtual Agents and Power BI.

In the rest of this book, we will dive deeper into how to leverage Dataverse features to design data models to solve real world business scenarios.

2

Common Data Model Overview

In the past when building an application, you would start with a clean slate and decide what tables, worksheets or lists made up your data model. This led to every application reinventing the wheel and resulted in not only wasted efforts but applications that had a difficult time talking to each other for integration, migration and sharing of logic.

Microsoft recognized this and Dynamics CRM/365 started to ship with a pre-built set of tables related to customer relationship management. This included tables like Contact, Account and Opportunity to name a few. While this was an improvement, it still required licensing the application to use the tables, and they were only intended to be used in the context of the Microsoft app.

As Microsoft Dataverse (at the time it was called Common Data Service) was initially released, Microsoft also separated out the data entity definitions into the first version of the Common Data Model. For the initial version this was influenced by Dynamics 365 table definitions but not completely aligned. Later as Dataverse evolved and took on more of the capabilities of the Dynamics 365 core data engine the Common Data Model evolved to be closer aligned. Today Dynamics 365 customer engagement applications run on Microsoft Dataverse and Dynamics 365 customer engagement apps no longer have their own core data engine.

Microsoft Dataverse

What is the Common Data Model?

The Common Data Model (CDM) is simply the entity definitions of commonly used business data. The CDM does not prescribe an implementation of the data processing engine itself, only a definition of what makes up the core definition of the entity. It's also important to note, that this does not preclude consumers of the CDM from extending the data model for their own business scenarios. In fact, one of the goals of CDM is to promote a core model that is common and can be counted on when you are working with a data source that implements that part of the CDM.

Dataverse represents a data service that implements the CDM, or at least part of it. When you create a new environment with Dataverse provisioned you get what is referred to as CDM core. If you license and install any of the Dynamics 365 customer engagement applications, you get additional parts of the CDM referred to as the CRM entity definitions. The following is a high-level illustration of those entities.

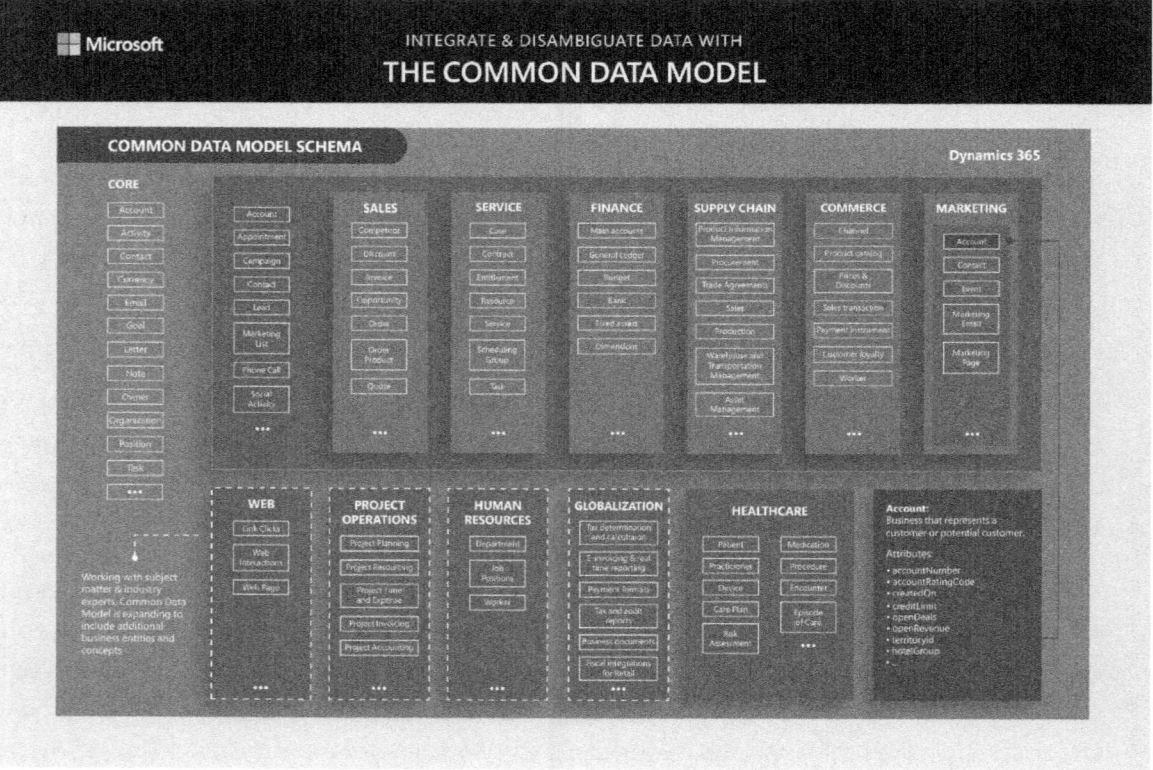

If Dataverse was the only use of the common data model it wouldn't make sense to separate it out into its own thing. Microsoft envisions the common data model being available for any data source to use to describe the data it contains. To help this along Microsoft has published the common data model on GitHub.com and licensed it under the Creative Commons Attribution 4.0 International Public License.

It is Microsoft's hope that with this open license, many will start using the CDM definitions as a starting point for their data definitions and therefore increase the interoperability of systems without complex mapping requirements.

To help this goal along, Microsoft has included as part of Power BI dataflows the ability to map an external non-CDM data source into a standard CDM entity. Power BI dataflows are a collection of data from various sources that facilitate getting data into Power BI storage for use by Power BI. This data is then stored in an Azure data lake and is available for processing as CDM structured data.

To give an example of this in action, if I were to take my data from my own internal system that was people data e.g., first name, last name etc. and bring that into a Power BI dataflow I could map that data to the CDM Contact entity. Then any Power BI dashboard or report built to work with CDM contact data could process that data.

Another example, if I still had a need to build an on-premise proprietary system, I could still use CDM. I wouldn't get the schema all created for me automatically like what happens with Dataverse when it uses CDM definitions, but as I modeled my tables in my local SQL store, I could model the data using the CDM core definitions. This would make my internal system easier to integrate with other CDM oriented tools and apps in the future.

Having a common data model also benefits end-users when a company has multiple systems or apps that use the same definitions it should be familiar to them as they access the apps.

Extending CDM for specific industries

The Common Data Model is intended to cover common concepts and activities used across business and productivity applications. Generally, the entities and associated definitions are not specific to individual industries. Microsoft however recognizes that many industry vertical solutions also have commonalities that could benefit from a similar concept and has released industry accelerators covering key areas.

The accelerators are not intended to be complete solutions, but a jump start to give ideas on what could be done and include a starter data model for the vertical. In each vertical, Microsoft has partnered with independent software vendors (ISVs) and other experts in that vertical to define the common concepts that make up CDM extensions.

Microsoft has published (or is in the process of publishing) accelerators for the following verticals:

- Banking
- Healthcare
- Education
- Nonprofit/charity
- Automotive
- Media

These CDM extensions are intended to be starting points for ISVs, partners, and customers that build in that vertical to further build on top of the CDM Extensions.

To give an example of the types of CDM extensions the accelerators define let's look at the healthcare accelerator entities. Unique to this accelerator are entities like patients, devices, care plans, observations, and practitioners to name a few.

If you are building an app in one of these verticals at a minimum you should evaluate if the accelerator offers anything to help jump start or inspire your app. Even if you can't directly use the same entity definitions, modeling as close as possible will be helpful for integration scenarios.

The accelerators can also serve as a learning tool for looking at how data modeling challenges have been solved. Often the same data modeling concepts can apply to other industries or business problems.

How to use the Common Data Model with Dataverse

Today there are two primary scenarios for leveraging CDM with Dataverse. The first is when you create a new environment with Dataverse provisioned you will get CDM core entities automatically provisioned as tables within Dataverse. You should become familiar with these tables and their purpose and when you have a scenario that matches their purpose you should prioritize reusing them rather than inventing your own table.

The second use case scenario is if you have any of the Dynamics 365 customer engagement apps, they will install the CDM CRM grouping of entity definitions as part of the apps. Unfortunately, today this is the only way to get these entity definitions and it requires a license to the Dynamics 365 apps. You also currently can't start with Dataverse with only the core entities and grow up to Dynamics 365. In the future, I'd like to see Microsoft separate the core parts of these entities and allow their installation as a CDM "Solution Package" on top of the core CDM schema that comes with new Dataverse environments. Until that happens, the best you can do is if you need/want to use one of the entities e.g., Opportunity is to look at the CDM definition and create your own custom table using as close to the same columns as possible. By at least keeping it as close as possible on the column names, today this will help keep mapping for integration scenarios minimal and in the future if those entities become available you could migrate easier to the official CDM definitions.

CDM on GitHub

The Common Data Model can be found on GitHub at https://github.com/microsoft/CDM .

Here you can find all the entity definitions and submit issues and change proposals. If you look at the raw CDM definition files for an entity they are stored in JavaScript Object Notation (JSON) which, while human readable, are more geared towards consumption by an application. You can see an example of the account entity here
https://github.com/microsoft/CDM/blob/master/schemaDocuments/core/applicationCommon/Account.0.8.1.cdm.json

A better way to browse the CDM definitions is to use the CDM Visual Entity Navigator. You can launch the navigator here https://microsoft.github.io/CDM/

Microsoft Dataverse

This tool allows you to visually explore the CDM definitions. For example, if you select account you would see the following:

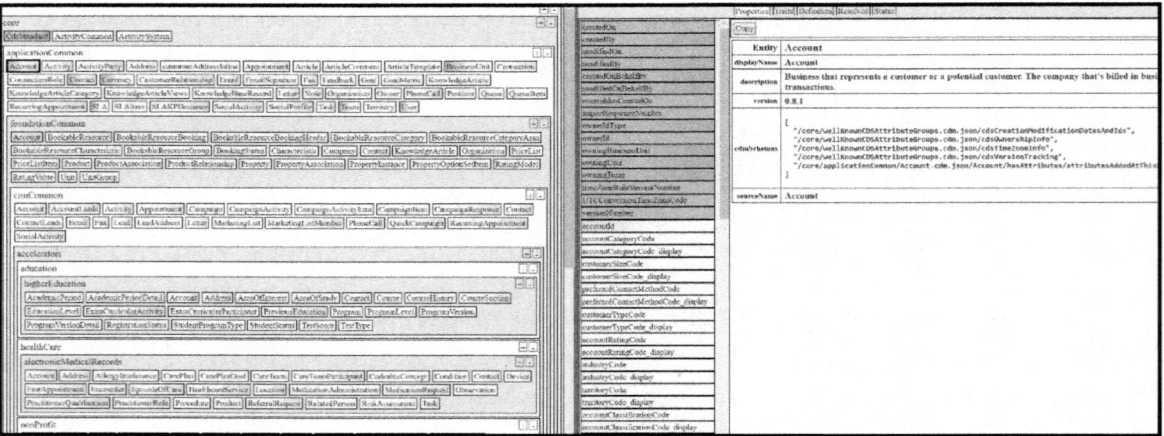

The left side highlights each of the CDM entities that have an interaction with account in some capacity. The middle column lists all the attributes. The right panel provides a description and standard display names for the entity.

The color highlights indicate the following:

Microsoft Dataverse

Color Key:
| Used by Selected | Uses the Selected | Base of Selected | Extension of Selected |

These can be used to explore how entities are used and extended across the different parts of the model. For example, account is extended by the accelerators and if you click on account you can see what is added by that CDM extension.

Clicking on one of the attribute names will show the following details for the attribute (field).

Attribute	accountNumber
displayName	Account Number
description	Type an ID number or code for the account to quickly search and identify the account in system views.
isPrimaryKey	false
dataFormat	String
maximumLength	20
isReadOnly	false
isNullable	true
creationSequence	43
sourceName	accountnumber
valueConstrainedToList	false

Included here is the dataFormat of the field. Keep in mind these do not use the same terminology as Dataverse for describing the data format / data type. You will learn more about Dataverse data types later in the content.

Getting to know the CDM Core entities

In this section we are going to look at some of the most used entities that are part of the CDM core. These entities are available in every Dataverse environment as tables and having a basic understanding of them is essential to building apps on the platform. A full list of the core entities can be found here https://docs.microsoft.com/en-us/common-data-model/schema//core/applicationcommon/overview

Entity - Account

CDM Definition: Business that represents a customer or a potential customer. The business could be billed as part of a business transaction.

Notable attributes:

- Account Number – This can be used as a way to lookup the account. Adding an alternate key to this can allow you to enforce uniqueness. You can also change this to auto number and have the account numbers generated using the pattern you choose.
- Address 1-3 fields – While these fields appear to be on the account entity the data is really stored as records of the Address entity.

Notable relationships:

- Accounts can have parent accounts and child accounts which can create a hierarchy of accounts.
- Accounts can have contacts associated with it both as the primary contact and as the company associated with a contact. One important thing to understand about the relationship form contact to account is the way it is configured if you delete an account all associated contacts are deleted as well. This behavior cannot currently be changed but one option is to not provide delete on account (using security roles) and force users to inactivate the records instead.

Entity - Address

CDM Definition: Address and shipping information. Used to store additional addresses for an account or a contact.

This is a special entity that is used to store the address data for accounts and contacts. Currently it is not available to create similar relationship with other entities.

Today, if you need your own address records or fields on an entity use this entities fields to model similar data types on your own custom entities/fields.

Entity - Activities

This collection of entities is intended to track interactions with related records. CDM's pre-defined activity entities are named appointment, email, FAX, letter, phone call, social activity and task. Later we will talk about how to define custom activities for other scenarios.

Activity entities are special in that they all inherit some fields from a generic Activity entity. For example, they all get subject and start time / end time and several other fields.

You can't directly create an activity entity record; it gets created for you by the system when you create one of the specific activity type records e.g. a phone call.

You can however get a list of all activity entity records regardless of type allowing applications to present timelines of interactions to app users. Users can then drill down to see specific activity type data.

Dataverse security for activities is all or nothing, you can't say a user can read phone call activities but not email activities. As you start thinking through how your security model works with your data model this might influence your use of activities.

To allow association of the activity with other records the regarding field is used. Regarding is a lookup field to other records but it is a special type of lookup field. This lookup field dynamically adjusts to allow setting it to any entity type that is enabled for activities.

Another notable relationship is to activity party. This is used to track things like sender and recipients of activities. An activity party points to a person or a group. The built-in activities like task, phone call and appointment each use a subset of the overall 11 activity party types that are supported. You can read more on the usage of activity parties here https://docs.microsoft.com/en-us/powerapps/developer/common-data-service/activityparty-entity

Entity - Business Unit

CDM Definition - Business, division, or department.

Business unit is a special entity and used as part of the security model. Typically, business unit records are created by system administrators. Essentially, they are used to group users and own records based on user/team assignment. Later we will talk about entity ownership, and when a record is owned by a user or team it is therefore owned by a business unit record.

While you could create records to match an organization hierarchy, generally it is best to use them to group users and allocate privileges from security roles to help you implement a security model. For example, let's say you had Contoso with a Sales business unit and it had Residential and Commercial child business units. You could leverage that for your security model to give a manager access to all of sales and your residential users would only have access to their residential records.

Entities - Connection and Connection Role

These entities are used to track informal relationships between entity records. We will be talking about these more in the relationship content.

Entity – Contact

CDM Definition - Person with whom a business unit has a relationship, such as a customer, a supplier, or a colleague.

If you are using Power Apps portals, contacts can represent external users and can be granted permissions to data the portal surfaces.

Contact and account entities are probably the most commonly reused entities by custom and ISV solutions. In fact, I challenge you to find a business problem that doesn't somewhere involve people or companies!

Notable attributes:

- Like account, the address fields are really stored as address entity records.
- Full Name – this is a composite field consisting of first and last name. In Dataverse, an environment wide setting determines the order of the full name (e.g. "First Last" or "Last, First")
- There is a collection of *do not allow* fields that can be helpful for honoring a contact's communication preferences.
- External user identifier can be used to connect to other systems including authentication identifiers. Keep in mind it has a default length of 50 which might need to be increased.

Notable Relationships:

- The default relationship to accounts only allows being associated with one account. If you need to support association with multiple accounts, consider using your own relationship.

Entity – Customer Relationship

While this entity is still in CDM for backward compatibility it has been deprecated and instead you should look at using connections. We will discuss this more later.

Entity – Currency

CDM Definition - Currency in which a financial transaction is carried out.

Any entity that has a currency data type field will have a relationship created to the currency entity. This entity is used to represent the currencies you can transact and store currencies in your data.

In Dataverse, you can't add additional columns to this table. If you have this need you could create a custom entity that had currency as a lookup and store the additional data there.

A common integration is to update the exchange rate attribute with the current conversion rate.

Entity – Feedback

CDM Definition - Container for feedback and ratings

Notable Attributes:

- Rating stores the rating a user provides. Min and max rating provide the available range, and normalized rating is a calculated value normalized by min/max.

Notable Relationships:

- The regarding relationship is configured for other entities allowing them to be set as the regarding record for feedback. By enabling *allow feedback* option on an entity it can be set as the regarding on a feedback record.

Entity – Note

CDM Definition - Note that is attached to one or more objects, including other notes.

This is used for capturing notes for other entities. It must be enabled for an entity which creates the relationship automatically between the note and the entity. You might also hear this entity referred to by its internal name of annotation.

You can use the note entity also to attach a file along with the note. For example, you could store a copy of a receipt or other static documentation related files. Keep in mind, Dataverse is reasonable for storing static files, but not intended to be a document management app like SharePoint with collaboration.

Notable Attributes:

- Object ID stores the ID of the related entity.
- Subject contains the title of the note.
- Note text stores the text of a note.
- IsDocument is used to identify if a note record has an attached file
- Document body stores the contents of an attached file and mime type indicates for format of that data. This data must be encoded into base 64 format and must be decoded prior to use by an application.

Entity - Position

CDM Definition - Position of a user in the hierarchy.

This entity is used by Dataverse to implement position-based hierarchal security. This allows security models to be built based on a position hierarchy instead of a reporting manager hierarchy.

When enabled, users assigned a position directly above another user's position will have read, write, update permissions to the user's data and those higher up the chain, will have read only access.

Notable Relationships:

- A user can be assigned a single position, but the position can be held by multiple users.

Entities - Queue and Queue Item

These entities are used queuing and routing work that needs to be completed. Queues can be used by a team of people to pick records that they then take ownership of to work on. For example, a new email was received and placed into a queue. The team assigned to work those emails could pick up the item from the queue which would make it unavailable for others and then proceed to do any work.

In Dataverse, you must enable table for queuing for the item to be eligible to be queued. When an item is queued, a queue item row is created to track the table row in the queue.

Entity – Team

Team is a special entity that is used as part of the security model to represent a collection of users. Teams can be of three types – owning teams, access teams and group teams. Teams are related to and exist in the context of a business unit. Every business unit has a default team that has its members automatically maintained by the system to equal any user that is assigned to that business unit. For the default team you can't manually change the member list like you can with other custom created teams.

Teams can have security roles associated with them granting its user members those permissions in the context of the team's business unit. Owning teams can own records of entities configured for user/team ownership. Access teams are used most commonly to dynamically assign access to a record to the team's members. This is done by setting up an Access Team Template (a set of permissions to grant) and then when a user is associated with the record a team is created on the fly, and the users added as members. This is used commonly when a dynamic team member list needs to be maintained per record. The final group team has an association with Azure Office/Security groups as a way to grant permissions to users and leverage Azure AD group membership to control Dataverse team membership.

Sometimes this concept of team can conflict with business application "team" concepts. For example, in sports you might have teams, you will not want to reuse the Dataverse team table and instead creating your own unique Sports Team. As tempting as it might be to just name it Team, and the system will let you – having two teams show up for users will be confusing!

Entity - User

The user entity is a special entity representing the system user. Most rows of this table in Dataverse are automatically created by the system to represent users that have access to the Dataverse environment and are synchronized from the associated Azure AD.

Each user is associated with a business unit record and gets permissions in the context of that. Users are associated with the default business unit team and can also be manually associated with any number of other teams from any business unit.

Application users are special user records that represent an application that a developer created to access the system. Like other users this can get permissions from security roles directly assigned or via teams. This type of user can't log in and is tied to an Azure AD application registration. This is most commonly used by integration or automation apps.

Another type of user you might encounter is commonly referred to as a "stub" user. They are often created to track ownership of historic data. These are no longer licensed users but still need to be in the system from a historical data migration.

Open Data Initiative

Parallel to the efforts to define the Common Data Model, Microsoft has partnered with Adobe and SAP to kick off the Open Data Initiative. Open Data Initiative is a jointly developed vision. The vision is stated as "... a platform for a single, comprehensive view of your data, bringing together and enriching data from all your lines of business, across all your systems to deliver real-time intelligence back into your applications and service"

The journey to this vision is just beginning, so as you can imagine the details are few. It's likely that this effort will help shape the Common Data Model and will drive interoperability of data across the participating vendor applications. Today participating vendors are the core, I suspect if it takes off to see others agree to participate. You can follow things as they develop here
https://www.microsoft.com/en-us/open-data-initiative

Wrapping it up

Having a good understanding of what makes up the core CDM entities and how Dataverse implements it as a table is essential to ensure you don't re-invent something you already have. Also, not repurposing a CDM entity is just as important because that makes it unavailable for its intended purpose.

The concept of having a Common Data Model is evolving so this is not a learn once and move on. Keep your eye on CDM evolution as it continues to mature.

3

Working with tables

In this chapter, we will dive deeper into creating tables and making choices for the associated options. Currently, the three most common ways to get a table defined in your environment is to have it when you create the environment because it was part of CDM core, install a solution that contains one or more tables, this includes installing an app from AppSource and manually creating a custom table. A reminder that tables used to be called entities so when you are reading content online that is older. In this content, we will try to only use entity to refer to the Common Data Model schema definitions.

Later we will talk about strategies for identifying what should be a table. For now, the primary choice we will consider is if you reuse an existing table or create it custom. The primary consideration for this should be does your use match the intended use for the existing table. The advantage of reuse of an existing, is two part. First, you save the time because many of the columns already are defined and second you get compatibility with anything that was built to use that pre-existing table. A great example of this is account and contact, if you reuse them for tracking people you instantly get access to most marketing applications.

The actual mechanics of creating a table are so simple it's easy to think why bother spending time thinking through any considerations. Even though easy to create, a table will be a part of your app that will remain around for years. Often shortcuts early lead to more rework later on. Just as you would have considerations on adding a room to your house, you should have similar considerations when adding a table to your system. Some things to consider:

- Does CDM already have a similar table we should consider reusing?
- Do we already have a custom table that is similar?
- Is there other data we might need to capture that is very similar?
- How does access to this data need to be controlled?
- Should this be a table – or is it better as a choice? (more on this later)
- Should we make the table more generic e.g., Products instead of Cooking Utensils? Or more specific?
- Is the name we plan to use unique enough compared to other tables we have or might have? E.g. Category vs Travel Category

You should also consider the following if you are thinking of reusing an existing table:

- Is our purpose similar to how it is intended to be used?
- Are there any data comingling restrictions that would prevent mixing the new data with existing?
- Is the table customizable enough to support our needs? (check if the table is fully enabled for customization)
- Is there automation built on the existing table that isn't compatible?

Naming Tables

When you create a new table, you will provide the following three names:

Property Name	Description
Display Name	This is the singular name that the user will see when they work with this table. This is not the name that developers will use but a name for the end user. For example, for a real estate system you might put Property to refer to the real estate property. Keep in mind you are allowed to have multiple tables with the same display name as long as the Name column is unique. To help users and yourself from getting confused try to keep Display Names unique as well. In our example of Property, that might mean naming it Real Estate Property if there was already a

	Property table.
Plural Name	This is the name used when there is a list or a grid of the table. Using our same real estate property example, you might put the word Properties in the plural to show to the user. This name will be pre-filled for you based on your Display Name, however, you can override it if you feel the system didn't do a good job of naming your table.
Name	This column is also pre-populated from your publisher prefix plus the display name. So, using our same example, if our publisher prefix was Contoso the name would be contoso_Property. Unlike the Display and Plural that can be changed at any time, this name column will become read-only after creation. This name is used by developers and keeping the name consistent after creation ensures any code using the name will not break.

Pro tip: If you can keep the names similar, you avoid the developer calling it a "Transaction" and the business user calling it a "Deal". In other words, leverage this capability when it makes sense but do not just have different names just because you can.

Primary Column

An often-overlooked key part of creating a custom table is the primary column. By default, if you don't do anything special this will be created as a column called "<prefix>_name" and will be of type single line of text. The primary column will show up in a few places with special meaning such as the title of the window when you view a record of that type. You cannot change the primary attribute after the initial creation other than the description and the constraints.

Consider if "Name" is the correct name or if Title or some other name is appropriate.

You can also change the requirement level of the column and the max length after creation of the table.

The display name for the primary column is also used for the unique ID column display name for the table. You can customize this e.g. instead of Name you could call it Student Key or Student ID if you want.

Enabling Notes and Attachments

This checkbox defaults to off and can be changed to on at any point. Enabling it creates a relationship from the custom table you are creating to the note table. You should only enable this when you need the ability to track notes and attachments. Once enabled you can't turn it off.

Table Type

There are three different types of tables. You can only create standard and activity tables from the maker portal. The following are the type of tables you can create:

Type	Description
Standard	This is the most common type of table and has no special capabilities.
Activity	This allows you to create custom activity types that behave like the CDM activity types e.g., task/phone call, etc. Activity tables are special because they can inherit standard activity attributes from the activity table and when you create a record it also maintains the activity record.
Virtual	These tables represent data that is stored externally or are otherwise materialized by a provider created by a developer. Many scenarios where this would be appropriate can now be handled using embedded canvas apps and connectors instead of having a developer create a virtual entity data provider. Virtual entities however are still supported and represent read-only data that is surfaced like other tables, but the data is not stored in Dataverse. To implement a virtual entity, you must have a data provider built by a developer to connect Dataverse to the external data.

Activities are special in that they all inherit columns from a common parent table called activity (internally called ActivityPointer). This special inheritance is only supported and used on the activity tables. When you create a task, an email or any of the other activity type tables, you are creating a row in the ActivityPointer table as well in the specific task or email table. This special inheritance relationship is important to understand because you will need to use it at times when retrieving data.

ActivityPointer itself is not customizable, but you can modify each of the inherited activity types. You can customize the views for ActivityPointer which are used when displaying lists of all different types of activities. Each activity can be customized to add columns and customize the forms/views. For example, if you wanted to add an column like Billable to each activity, you can't just add it to ActivityPointer, you would have to add it to task, email, letter, and so on, each individually.

Custom Activities

Custom activities allow you to create your own activity from scratch and have it participate in the system like built-in activities do. A simple example might be to track instant messages between an agent and a contact, or possibly to track text messages sent.

Creating a custom activity is just like creating any custom table with the exception you need to mark it as an activity at the time of creation. This means that you can't decide later you want to activate a table as an activity it must be done at the time of creation. In the same token, you cannot take a standard table and make it an activity one.

Custom activities start with all the same attributes from ActivityPointer and then any that you create custom. They have their own form so you can customize it as needed. That also means you can have Power Automate flows or developer created automation that run for custom activity events. For example, back to the text message custom activity you might have a developer created plugin that on create or update of a publish column sends it to an external service that sends text messages. Twitter is another easy example where that type of integration works well. Then you can send text messages or tweets from a flow.

One key thing to consider about custom activities, they don't get their own security role settings. All security for all activities is controlled together. For example, if you have permission to create or modify an activity you can create or modify any activity.

Table Row Ownership

Ownership indicates who owns the rows of data created in the table. If you are creating data related to users that they should own, then user/team ownership is correct. The other option is organization-owned, this is great for configuration data or other data that is not specific to a user. For example, we wrote an import utility that needed some configuration settings, having those tables be organizationally owned made a lot of sense. On the other hand, if you want to have a record owned by a specific user or team, then user or team-based ownership makes more sense. This cannot be changed after the table has been created, therefore if you aren't sure your needs choosing user/team owned should be your default choice.

Collaboration Options

These are a set of options you can configure when creating or modifying a table that all relate to collaboration on the data. The most important thing to notice on these options is many of them once turned on can't be turned off later. All options in this section generally are best left off unless you need the feature. Remember, all of these can be enabled after creation, so you don't have to feel obligated to enable upon creation.

Option	Description
Allow feedback	Enabling this creates a relationship to the feedback table. Enable this when you want capture feedback related to your custom table records. We discussed the feedback table already in more detail with CDM.
Enable as activity task	This allows you to track activities against the custom table by setting the regarding property on the activity. There is not currently a way to limit which activities can be related, enabling this allows any activity type to be related to your custom table.
Send email to table	Enabling this will allow users to send email to the table, in a model-driven application the send email button will light up. If the table has an email column, it will be used, if not one will be created when this option is enabled. An example of where this might be useful, imagine you created a student table instead of using contact, enabling this option would allow emails to be sent to the student using the built-in email support.
Support mail merge	This enables the table to be used for Microsoft Word mail merge – can be changed at any point and is primarily used for legacy mail merge support that is being retired. There are more modern capabilities like document generation and Microsoft Word connectors for Power

	Automate that will be taking its place.
SharePoint document management	This currently only fully works if you have one of the Dynamics 365 customer engagement apps installed. The option also requires server-side SharePoint integration to be enabled for the environment. This allows SharePoint documents to be related to your table record.
Auto-create access teams	This allows use of dynamic access teams and should only be enabled when you need to dynamically grant permissions to the record for a team that differs from record to record.
Enable Queues	This enables support for association of table records with queues. This is useful for workload management of incoming work. Once turned on table rows can be placed in any available queue.

Create and Update settings

The following settings can be changed at any point in time.

Option	Description
Enable quick create	This works in conjunction with creating a quick create form for a table to provide a streamlined creation experience. This is best used when creating does not require the full set of columns. To have quick create work, you must have this enabled, have a quick create form and have included the quick create form in your model-driven app.
Duplicate detection	Enabling this option will allow duplicate detection rules to be created to attempt to identify duplicates. Duplicates can be checked via the model-driven apps as well as by developers using the API.
Enable change tracking for flow	While this label includes flow in the title, the current versions of the flow triggers for Dataverse don't require it to be enabled. Enabling this option however does still enable change tracking that developers can use via the API to retrieve records created, modified or deleted since the last check. This is useful for integration scenarios where you only want to

process changes. This feature is also used by the Data Export to Azure Data Lake to allow incremental updates from Dataverse.

Offline settings

The following settings can be changed at any point in time.

Option	Description
Enable for mobile offline	This allows users of a model-driven app to use the table when offline.
Enable Dynamics 365 Outlook offline capabilities.	This table is enabled or disabled for offline capabilities in Dynamics 365 for Outlook. This is in support of the COM add-in that was retired in 2020. You should not need this for newer apps.

The Built-In Columns

When you complete the initial table property form, and the system creates the custom table it also creates a few columns for you by default. These are used by the platform to manage instances of the table and can't be removed.

A common mistake of new makers is creating their own columns instead of taking advantage of the built-in columns that are already maintained by the system.

The following table shows the columns that are created by default each time.

Column Name	Description
CreatedBy	Unique identifier of the user who created the record.
CreatedOn	Date and time when the record was created.
CreatedOnBehalfBy	This stores the user who created record if impersonation was being

	used this will represent the real user.
ID	Unique identifier for table instances, the real name for this is <prefixname>_<tablename>id. This is a GUID and is used to reference this table in the future using the API.
Importsequencenumber	Sequence number of the import that created this record. This is useful if you are doing research on how data was input into the system to determine if it was an import problem.
ModifiedBy	Who did the last modification to this record?
ModifiedOn	When was the last modification done?
ModifiedOnBehalfBy	This stores the user who modified record if impersonation was being used this will represent the real user.
Ownerid	This is the id of the user/team that is the current owner of the record. The user can only be an owner of records that security provides access to. Owner ID is changed when a record is assigned to another user. Records that have an ownership type of organization will not have this attribute added during creation because there is no user that owns those records.
Owningbusinessunit	The business unit that owns this record. This attribute will be automatically set by the system based on the owner of the record.
OwningTeam	If owned by a team this will contain the lookup value of the team.
OwningUser	If owned by a user, this will contain the lookup value of the user.
Statuscode	Status of the table instance maintained by the system. For most tables this is Active or Inactive.
Statusreason	This is the reason describing the status. E.g. Inactive and Expired where expired would be the reason. Most tables allow customizing of these values which default to Active and Inactive like the status.

Wrapping it up

Before rushing out to create a custom table taking a few minutes to evaluate existing tables is essential. In this chapter we looked at some of the considerations when creating tables. We also established some considerations to review prior to creation. Later we will continue to explore things to consider when putting together a data model and how best to leverage custom tables.

4

Working with columns

In this chapter, we will dive deeper into creating columns and how to choose the data type that is appropriate for your data. While the key choice you are making on a column is called data type you are really choosing a data type and formatting at the same time. This choice can enforce constraints on the data you store in the column and care should be taken to ensure the right choice is made.

Some of the choices you make can't be changed after creation. For example, if you choose text, you can later change it to auto number and apply some automation to generate the text value. On the other hand, you can't change the text column to a whole number.

For existing tables, you can make limited changes to the existing columns. For example, if there is a more commonly accepted display name that matches your company vocabulary you can simply change an existing column display name. Watch out when reusing columns to ensure your use is consistent with the intent. You shouldn't feel bad that there are some columns on the existing tables that you aren't using because you created custom columns.

When adding a column to a table you should consider the following:

- Is there an existing column on the table with the same purpose (if so, reuse it!)?

- If there is an existing column, is the data type correct for your needs?
- Do you know enough about the data you will be storing to choose the data type and formatting?

Custom Columns

Adding additional columns to an out of the box table or adding a new one to a custom table is the same process so this section will apply to both. Columns that are added to a table are then available to be added to the table's main form to allow the user to modify and view the contents. It is not required that all columns are added to the table form, in fact it is common to have columns that are used by custom business logic extensions and never shown to the end user.

When you create a new column the most important decision is the data type of column. Once created, you cannot change the data type. The only way you "change" the data type is to delete and re-create the column. It's not difficult to imagine the challenges this presents when the data you are changing is already deployed to users.

There are over 25 different data type/formats that can be used on columns. You can find the current list of supported types here https://docs.microsoft.com/en-us/powerapps/maker/common-data-service/types-of-fields. Some of these can only be used/created by the system. In this module, we are going to only highlight the most common ones and some of the key things to be aware of when creating the columns.

Text Columns

Text columns are probably the most common and safe choice for a column. If you choose text, the most important thing to be aware of is it can hold only up to 4,000 characters. If you are working with a long narrative, a safer choice is to choose multiline text which can hold up to 1,048,576 characters. The length can be increased at any point in time up to the column's limit.

Don't confuse text area with multiline text. Text area is just like text but when used with model-driven will provide a text area for input instead of just a single line. Generally, text is good for short title and labels, text area is good for a brief description and multiline is good for a long narrative.

It's also tempting to cheat and make columns text that will store numbers. Doing this messes up sorting and also doesn't give you the proper formatting of the number. You also lose the ability to specify minimum and maximum values for the number, and it limits the ability to use the data in math without extra conversion of the data.

While making columns text is quick and easy take the time to understand your data. This also might require you to do some data cleansing of your existing data to remove values that aren't valid that might have made it into your old system that didn't have proper data validation.

Also available as text columns are email, URL, phone, auto number and ticker symbol. These are simply formatting, validation and special rendering on a text data type. Be sure if you use these that you can live with the formatting and validation rules that are specific to that format. For example, if in a column with URL formatting you needed to store a relative URL and not a fully qualified URL you would be stuck. All of them except for auto number can't be changed after initial creation. Text can be changed to auto number at any time, and an auto number can be changed back to text.

Auto number columns can be very helpful to assign human readable generated values. These can then be given to a customer so when they contact you back, they can provide the value making it easier to lookup the record in the system. Auto numbers can be string, date or custom prefixed. When using custom, you choose the pattern to use. The following are some examples of how you could build the custom format pattern:

Pattern	Example value
CAR-{SEQNUM:3}-{RANDSTRING:6}	CAR-123-AB7LSF
CNR-{RANDSTRING:4}-{SEQNUM:4}	CNR-WXYZ-1000
{SEQNUM:6}-#-{RANDSTRING:3}	123456-#-R3V
KA-{SEQNUM:4}	KA-0001
{SEQNUM:10}	1234567890
QUO-{SEQNUM:3}#{RANDSTRING:3}#{RANDSTRING:5}	QUO-123#ABC#PQ2ST
QUO-{SEQNUM:7}{RANDSTRING:5}	QUO-0001000P9G3R

Microsoft Dataverse

Pattern	Example value
CAS-{SEQNUM:6}-{RANDSTRING:6}-{DATETIMEUTC:yyyyMMddhhmmss}	CAS-002000-S1P0H0-20170913091544
CAS-{SEQNUM:6}-{DATETIMEUTC:yyyyMMddhh}-{RANDSTRING:6}	CAS-002002-2017091309-HTZOUR
CAS-{SEQNUM:6}-{DATETIMEUTC:yyyyMM}-{RANDSTRING:6}-{DATETIMEUTC:hhmmss}	CAS-002000-201709-Z8M2Z6-110901

Number Columns

Whole number columns are also commonly used. Things like number of children or years in column are great examples of whole number columns. Wait a second not so fast! You have to be careful. For example, years in column only is good if we want to round up or down if you have a partial year. If you needed to say 17.5 years, then decimal number would be a better choice. This requires you to know your data and potential future data. If you think you might need decimal points, lean towards that now, you can always round up/down but you can't add precision to a whole number later without re-creating the column and migrating old data. If you don't want to show the decimals you can control that on display of the data.

Other whole numbers types are duration, time zone and language. These are just formats on a whole number column that aren't changeable after creation. They are useful, for example for our event management app. We have the date/time as time zone independent and have an additional column of type time zone that stores the time zone separately. This allows us to clearly communicate to the form user what time zone the event is in. In model-driven apps, duration, time zone and language columns provide rich controls for input. For example, time zone provides a drop-down list of all the time zones.

Pro tip: *Always check advanced options on whole numbers you can set the min and max value range. This is an easy way to validate users input the right range of values without having to create custom logic to validate the ranges. If you need more dynamic values based on other criteria, consider business rules.*

In addition to whole numbers there are also decimal and floating-point types. Each of these supports storing a decimal point determined by a configured precision. The difference between the two is decimal stores the exact value, while floating point stores an extremely close approximation. I generally prefer to use decimal if I need more than a whole number.

Currency Columns

The currency type should always be used to track monetary amounts. While it is true you could simply use a decimal column, currency columns provide better support. When you create the first currency column on a table two additional columns are added. A currency lookup column is added to indicate the transactional currency of the record. Additionally, an exchange decimal column is added to store the last known exchange rate for the currency against the environment's base configured currency. This is a powerful feature if in today's global business world, you find yourself dealing with multi-currency transactions. It's good to remember this when you are building reporting because it allows you to produce a report on the base currency value without having to do the calculations row by row.

Pro tip: *The system will store the conversation rates you provide. It does not automatically seek the most current conversation rates. You can integrate with one of several available services to keep rates current if that's what is required.*

Date/Time Columns

Tracking when something occurred is probably one of the most important pieces of data you will capture. Dates can enable much of your automation and insights from your data. For example, they can allow you to automate follow up actions after a specific number of days or be used to gain insight on the average time your customer takes for some behavior. Don't hesitate to add more dates to your data model as long as you commit to keep them populated and accurate.

One of the common mistakes new people make with Dataverse is not realizing it already tracks created on and modified on for you, so you don't need to add your own columns for that. Also be aware if you are migrating historical data you can use the override created on (overridecreatedon) column to store a historical date. This can only be done during record creation.

When adding new date/time columns you basically make two key choices. First is this a date only column or date and time? Second is the behavior of the column and you can choose from user local, date only or time-zone independent?

Let's dig in a little deeper. First, it's important to understand that Dataverse stores date/time columns always in universal coordinated time (UTC). This works out great if you happen to have all your customers and users in that time zone, otherwise be prepared to at some point in your app do some time zone conversions.

That is a good place to explain some of the behaviors. The default behavior on date columns is user local. When this is set Power Apps model-driven apps automatically convert the date and time to the user's local time zone. With Power Apps canvas apps for any automation done with Power Automate you would need to do your own conversion of these dates. The same is true for developers working with the data directly via the API.

For date only columns, you can change behavior to date only and the time portion will always have a value of 12:00 am.

The final option is time-zone independent. This causes Power Apps model-driven apps to do no time-zone conversion before presenting the data to the user.

Date only columns are great for milestones when you don't care about a specific time. For example, a birthday, the hire date of an employee, essentially anything that is not tracked down to the minute.

Using the time-zone independent option is great when you need to stabilize the time for all users in all time-zones. I used the example earlier of the time an event starts. In our use we paired that date/time column with a time-zone column to make it clear what users were looking at.

For existing columns that are customizable, you can do a one-time change from user local to date only or time-zone independent. Just make sure you know how all apps use the data. You can read more on the conversion here https://docs.microsoft.com/en-us/dynamics365/customer-engagement/developer/behavior-format-date-time-attribute#convert-behavior-of-existing-date-and-time-values-in-the-database .

Choice (formerly Option Set)

Think of choice as a super dropdown list. Simply put, a choice is associated with a set of values and corresponding labels that can be picked by the user. Unlike a dropdown in a simple custom application, a choice column is fully integrated with the multi-language capabilities of the platform. For each configured language you can specify a display label that will show for that selected value.

When you create a choice column you can choose from any of the existing choice lists or create a new one. It's important that when you create a new one you give it a good name. While it might be a list of categories, that would be a terrible name for the choice list, what happens when you have another set of unrelated categories? You want to give as descriptive of a name as possible e.g. travel categories to ensure that when someone is looking at the list to reuse them, they aren't confused seeing three sets all named category.

If you choose to modify an existing choice list so you can use it, make sure you understand how it is already used as you could be impacting other apps. When you add new items to an existing choice list you can set the display label, and the numeric value that represents that option will be calculated for you using the choice prefix value from your solution publisher.

It might be obvious, but I will say it anyway, keep your list of choices to a reasonable amount. If you start getting over 100 values, you might consider other options like having a lookup column.

Choices (Formerly Multi-Select)

Columns using this data type also leverage the same choice lists we discussed above. The difference is these store multiple selected values. While this sounds great at first, be cautious of using multi-select because they don't have full support for easily doing low-code logic on the columns. For example, you can't use them in business rules or workflow. Overtime, these will likely gain full platform support but until then do your homework on how you plan to consume and interact with the column. When using a model-driven app, the columns are full featured for the user experience and work well. So, if you just need to capture data things will go smoothly, it's just a matter of how you wish to use the data that might be more complicated. When working with the columns from other apps or flows or developer API, the values for multi-select columns are stored as comma separated list of the numeric values. So, your logic will need to take on the consumption and label determination for using the columns.

Yes/No (Formerly Two Options)

Another option you have is to use the Yes/No data type. This data type is just like it sounds; two options, however you can control the label that shows. It could be yes or no (the default) or high/low, or any two values you like. The most important thing to think about is if you ever need to track a 3rd value. You can of course have a null value represent not provided but in some scenarios that is different than unknown. There is no way to take a yes/no column and make it a full choice column that has many values. If you think you might need more start with a choice column instead of a yes/no data type.

Lookup Columns

You might have noticed you can create lookup columns from the add column dialog. These essentially create a N:1 relationship to another table. I generally don't recommend creating the relationship from here because of the limited options it allows you to configure on the relationship. I recommend using the add relationship dialog which accomplishes adding the same lookup column but allows you to fully evaluate the options on your relationship without taking what Microsoft thinks are good defaults for every lookup column. We will cover lookup columns and N:1 relationship later on.

Other Column Properties

There are a couple of other choices you can make; searchable and required.

Searchable

This allows you to determine if a column appears in the model-driven Advanced Find. A good use for this is for hiding columns that aren't intended to be used by end-users.

Required

Columns can have three requirement levels: not required, business recommended, and required. The Power Apps portal does not let you set business recommended but you may encounter it on some older apps you look at. Required enforces data be input on a model-driven app but doesn't enforce that with other automations or apps. Business rules that are created and configured to run in the table scope can be used to enforce required data across all uses if you have that requirement.

Calculated and Rollup Columns

Internally, Dataverse has three types of columns simple, calculated and rollup. Simple columns are what we've been spending most our time talking about. Calculated columns are columns with values that are determined by a simple formula using data related to that table. Rollup columns are aggregates most commonly determined by counting or aggregating related records that match the provided criteria.

Calculated and rollup columns are similar in that they are both read only. They differ in how they are updated. Values for calculated columns are updated on retrieve of the record data from Dataverse. That means if the values making up the calculation change the calculated value is only updated on next retrieve of the data by any app. Rollup columns are mass calculated initially after 12 hours, and then by default a system job incrementally updates changed values every hour. Users of model-driven apps or developers via the API can request a single record column value be updated on demand.

Depending on the data type, calculated column formulas can concatenate values, do basic math on values. The biggest limitation of calculated columns is they can't use values from related records. You can read more about calculated columns here https://docs.microsoft.com/en-us/dynamics365/customer-engagement/customize/define-calculated-fields .

Rollup columns most commonly work against related data, but nothing requires you limit it just to related records. Values are calculated using sum, count, min, max or avg against a column on source record. For example, what is the most recent outage reported by a customer. Or what is the average order amount. You can read more about rollup columns here https://docs.microsoft.com/en-us/dynamics365/customer-engagement/customize/define-rollup-fields .

From a security point of view one thing to be aware of is both calculated and rollup column updates run at the system access level and if you have secured records or column security the calculated values can include data that the user wouldn't otherwise have access to. Sometimes this is the desired outcome, but it is good to be aware of the possible leakage of sensitive data.

The most common reason people get in trouble for using calculated or rollup columns is around the ability to immediately update the value. Make sure before settling on one of these columns that you don't have a scenario where you need instant visibility to the calculated value. For Power Apps canvas apps sometimes a formula in the app is a better choice and for Power Apps model-driven apps a business rule can sometimes be better.

Power Fx Formula Columns

Formula columns are a new type of Dataverse column data type that is currently in preview. Formula columns use Power Fx expressions to calculate a value in real time based on any of the columns on the table row. For example, you could have a formula column Discount Amount that used the expression Price * Discount. The data type of the column is dynamically determined based on the data type of the resulting expression. The result of the formula is evaluated upon retrieval of the row by an app, connector or API. Formula columns are currently only available in Microsoft Dataverse for Teams and not in full Dataverse environments.

Wrapping it up

It is easy to create columns and too often we jump quickly into bulk creating what we think we need without giving proper thought to the choices we make. A good example of bulk creating would be how Dataflows allow you to create columns inferring the data type. Columns like tables are part of the foundation of the apps you build. Changes to key things like data types can require costly rework if you make the wrong choices. Spend some time getting to know not only the new data your app will be collecting, but the historical data that will need to be migrated into your new Dataverse environment upon cutover from the existing system.

5

Relationships

Relationships are an important part of the data modeling capabilities of the platform because they allow you to further model real world situations. Relationships connect one table to another and define the characteristics of the relationships. In addition, by defining behaviors, automated actions can be configured to occur in conjunction with platform operations. Without this capability, our data would just be islands of information without meaningful connection.

A classic example of relationships would be an account having one or more contacts. That same account could also have a single primary contact. Another example would be an event having sessions, and sessions have a speaker. That example demonstrates some of the relationship questions that come up like "Is there one speaker or multiple?". As you work through data modeling these inquisitive questions and their answers shape the relationships you build.

In addition to just symbolic connecting of the dots between tables, relationships also result in some level of user interaction in Power Apps model-driven apps. Relationship definitions also contain behavior details that can help automate actions like deleting all child rows when a parent row is deleted. As an example, users will see this as they interact with lookup columns on forms, which are a representation of a relationship between two tables. They will also see changes take place to navigation and to their ability to view data all because of the relationships that exist. As part of building the model-driven app you have the ability to allow custom ordering and determination of how relationships are shown in the user interface.

From a developer perspective, relationships are also important because they define the navigation paths that you can use to query and find related data. Looking at relationships from a database perspective you would accomplish a similar task with foreign keys. Power Apps canvas app makers can also leverage relationships to traverse data as the user interacts with their app.

Relationships can be one of the more challenging areas of the platform to understand. Unlike other platform concepts, relationships have an impact several places and at times it can be challenging to understand why they work the way they do.

Microsoft Dataverse supports two types of relationships one-to-many or many-to-many. You may also see many to one mentioned this is just looking at a one-to-many relationships starting at the other table.

One-to-many

One-to-many relationships are hierarchical in nature and define a parent/child relationship. These relationships are often referred to as 1:N where N is the child or primary and related where N is the related. If you looked at it from the child perspective it would be N:1, but either way describing the same relationship just from the child's perspective.

Relationships with a cardinality of one-to-many are commonly used in solutions. For example, if we were modeling a hospitality solution (e.g., hotels) you might have a hotel table and it would be related the hotel room table. Each hotel could have multiple hotel rooms, but a hotel room only exists in a single hotel, or in relationship-speak it has a single parent. When you create one-to-many relationships, the child table gets a new lookup column added to its list of columns. This lookup column is the pointer to the "1" part of the relationship. In our hospitality example, room would have a lookup column named hotel that would be a pointer to the hotel that the room belongs with.

The following diagram is another example, where we are data-modeling a book. The book has chapters, and the chapters have pages. There is a one-to-many relationship between book and chapter and another one from chapter to page. These relationships result in a lookup column tracking the book id (dave_bookid) being added to the chapter list of columns. Similarly, a lookup column is added to page to point to the chapter id (dave_chapterid).

Book	Chapter	Page
PK dave_bookid	PK dave_chapterid	PK dave_pageid

A key thing to understand is that because of that lookup column pointing to the primary record, the same relationship can't be used to have a chapter be part of multiple books. At most the chapter can only be related to a single book. This is concept that even experienced people can get into trouble with where they model a one-to-many that really should be some form of many-to-many.

Many-to-many

Relationships that are many-to-many allow the ability to relate one item to multiple items, and that one item to be linked to multiple items of the same table type.

For example, we could define a custom table called language and it would contain all the possible languages people could speak. If we were to relate that to the contact table, we could then be able to relate to a contact all the languages they spoke. One person could speak English, French and German and have all of them tracked.

Using the many-to-many we could look at this relationship both ways – meaning we could ask the question what languages does this contact speak? Or the other direction what people speak this language?

Using our book example, imagine if we wanted to categorize the book. Most likely we wouldn't want our book to be in a single category we would want it to have many categories and we would use a many-to-many relationship to facilitate that. The following diagram shows what this might look like:

[Diagram: Book table (PK dave_bookid) — many-to-many — Category table (PK dave_categoryid)]

Internally, Dataverse maintains a joining table or sometimes referred to as a linker or intersect table. This table is maintained by the system and keeps a pointer to each record that is part of the many-to-many relationship. Currently, this table is not customizable to provide a place to store data (additional attributes) about the relationship. For example, it's not possible to track how long the person has spoken the language or how proficient they are in a language.

Manual many-to-many patterns vs. built-in many-to-many
One of the ways commonly used to overcome the limitation of the built-in many-to-many relationship of not tracking data about the relationship, is to create your own intersect table.

In this pattern a custom table is created with the sole purpose to have relationships to the other two tables that you want to have the many-to-many relationship between. The advantage of this pattern is that you can also add additional attributes to the "linker" or "intersect" table that describe the relationship. For example, you could indicate time frames that the relationship existed or a date the relationship expires. The disadvantage of this pattern is that it is much clumsier for the user to establish the relationship because there's no specific built-in UI to handle this type of many-to-many. Some of this can be overcome in the Power Apps built to consume the data.

Using our same book example from above, let's say we wanted to mark one of the categories as primary along with storing other columns like that about the relationship. The following diagram illustrates creating the book category table that has a many to one to both book and category and also provides the storage of the primary category column.

```
┌─────────────────┐      ┌──────────────────────┐      ┌─────────────────┐
│      Book       │      │    Book Category     │      │    Category     │
├─────────────────┤      ├──────────────────────┤      ├─────────────────┤
│ PK  dave_bookid │──o──o┤ PK  dave_bookcategoryid├o──o┤ PK  dave_categoryid│
└─────────────────┘      │     dave_primary     │      └─────────────────┘
                         └──────────────────────┘
```

Careful consideration should be given during establishment of many-to-many relationships to think about how it will be used in the future. Once in use, the only way to convert built-in many-to-many to a manual many-to-many pattern is manual, there is no automation provided. The same is also true if you implement the manual many-to-many pattern and your users aren't happy with the extra work.

Allowable Relationships

All custom tables you create can by default participate in one-to-many and many-to-many relationships. Tables from CDM or another ISV solution generally are available also, however, they can be locked down using managed properties. As a general rule, if you didn't create the table always check its ability to be customized before committing to its use in your solution.

Self-Referencing Relationships

Self-referencing allows a table such as an account to be related to another account record. This self-referencing creates a hierarchy of records. In fact, one relationship per table can be marked as hierarchical. This allows model-driven apps to have a built-in visualization and navigation of the set of records without any custom code.

Multiple Relationships

You can create multiple relationships between the same types of tables. For example, using our hotel room example I could add a relationship to a user called housekeeper and another one for maintenance person. This basically creates the two relationships between our hotel room table and the system user table.

Special Relationships

The following are some special relationships that enable some of the Dataverse related functionality.

Type	Description
Activity	This relationship is created by the system when you check the activity check box on the custom table definition. It is used to relate activities like task, email etc., to your custom table. This is system created and there is no way to create multiple activity type relationships. You can enable this at any time, but once this is enabled there is no way to disable for a table. The relationship is often referred to as the regarding relationship named after the lookup column on the activity. The regarding column is special because it can be associate an activity with any table in the environment that has activities enabled. This is different than a standard N:1 that only allows one specify table type to be related.
Notes	Note relationships are created by checking the notes check box on a custom table definition. The relationship allows tracking notes related to that custom table. This is created by the system and you can't create your own extra notes type relationships. You can enable this at any time, but once this is enabled there is no way to disable for a table.
Customer	The customer relationship type allows you to relate the record to a contact or an account. This allows you to create lookups to either an account or a contact, you can't add other table types.

Relationship Behaviors

One of the most important things to configure when you are creating a one-to-many relationship is the behavior of the related record when an action is performed on the primary record. The default relationship behavior is to simply remove the reference. So, for example you had a time sheet table that had time sheet items related to it, if you removed a time sheet record the default behavior would leave all the time sheet items in the system. These records would be orphaned in the system and that clearly is not in the best interest of managing the data.

When you create a relationship, look at the advanced section to configure relationship behaviors. Failing to consider this with every relationship you create is irresponsible. This is also the reason I don't recommend creating lookup columns using the "Add Column" as it does not make it obvious you need to set the behavior on the relationship.

The following are the different types of relationship behaviors and explain some automatic behaviors that get configured with each type.

Type	Description
System	These relationships are created by Dataverse and can't be modified or removed.
Parental	This creates a parent/child relationship. A table can only have a single relationship marked as parental but can have other relationships that are referential. Using our hotel example, the hotel would be the parent to the hotel room table. This makes sense because a hotel room would never exist without a hotel. If the parent is deleted, assigned, or shared then the child records are also affected. For example, if we deleted the hotel all hotel rooms would be deleted.
Referential	Referential relationships are common where the data is related but you don't want actions on the related record to affect the other. For example, where we related a category to a hotel room as to indicate the type of the room category. If the category was removed, we don't want to remove the hotel room we just want to remove the link. The same is true of assignment and sharing – they will not cascade to referential related records.

On this behavior you can also set it to restrict delete which allows you to prevent deletion of a primary record as long as related data exists. |
| Custom | Custom is the most flexible in that it lets you fully configure all the options that happen when the primary record is affected. See the following table on cascade types for the detail options that must be |

| | chosen for this type of behavior. |

Actions

The following are the different types of platform actions that can occur and allow you to specify a cascade type for each. These are used in conjunction with the custom option above. Each of these should be considered carefully during data model design time to evaluate what your requirements are when each action is performed.

Action	Description
Assign	This action occurs when you change the owning user of a user owned table. A common example of assign is changing the owner from Dave to Mary. Specification of cascade types on this option can control things such as if all related data should be assigned as well.
Share	This action occurs when data is shared with another user.
Unshare	Opposite of share, it allows specification if an unshared operation should cascade.
Reparent	Allows specification of how reparent should be controlled. CRM Tip of the day provides a good explanation of this in Tip # 184 https://crmtipoftheday.com/189/what-does-reparent-mean/
Delete	This is important because it controls how cascading works during a delete. By configuring this you can choose to cascade the delete, restrict the delete or simply remove the link. Restrict the delete requires the user to reassign all child records prior to deleting the related record.
Merge	Merge occurs when you combine multiple records together and what should happen to the children.

The following cascade types are used in conjunction with the actions above. For each action when using custom configuration, you will pick a cascade type to use for that particular action on the specific table.

Cascade Type	Description
Cascade All	This causes application of the operation to the current table and all related table rows.
Cascade Active	This only cascades the operation to related records that are active. This is common when using the assign action above to allow only records that are active to be assigned. Any retired record with a status of inactive would stay with the prior owner.
Cascade User Owned	This is powerful because it allows cascading the action against only records owned by the same user. For example, I might want a user to re-assign only the child records automatically with assignment of the parent if that user was the owner previously.
Cascade None	Cascade none prevents any of the actions for cascading down to related items.
Restrict	This is the same as specifying restricted referential. Basically, it keeps a delete from happening as long as there is related data. This only applies to use on the delete action dropdown.

Connections

Connections are a built-in Dataverse concept, allow a more dynamic representation of relationships between data. Typical N-1, 1-N, N-N type relationships are statically defined as part of metadata. Connections are more data driven and designed to be created or modified well after the initial solution is created or installed.

Connections work by using connection roles. Connection roles define one end of the connection and can also specify which table they can be used with and what connection roles can be used on the other end of the connection. For example, employee and employer are examples of two of the out of the box connection roles provided. Connection roles, however, can be included as part of a solution.

You can locate the list of connection roles by either going to the default solution -> connection roles or by looking at them in settings -> business management.

One advantage of connection roles for occasional relationships is it doesn't build any special data structure. Once connection roles are enabled for a table the relationship is created and you can use connections. While you can't turn off connections, you can ensure that no connection roles are configured for your table if you would like to minimize their future use.

The disadvantage of connections is the default user experience is poor and most users struggle to figure out how to connect the records. This can be overcome if you are comfortable creating a little bit of customization either via an embedded Power Apps canvas app or with the Power Apps Component Framework. Using these approaches, you can take complete control over the user experience. Another consideration is that all uses of connections get the same permission, so if you can see one type of connections you have permission to see all types of connections even if you don't have access to the related records.

Connections can be used as part of views and queries to filter data. For example, if you tag all your past employees you could do a query looking for contacts that had a tag of past employee.

Multi-table lookups preview

A long asked for Dataverse feature multi-table (polymorphic) lookups is now in preview. Traditionally look up columns are where a relationship is between one table type and another single table type. For example, an Order Item table that had a many-to-one relationship to a Product table. Imagine though if you sold both digital products and physical products and each of those types had different data columns that you needed to track. The multi-table lookup feature would allow you to have two or more tables (digital products and physical products) as the target of the relationship. When used in an app, a user could select a row from either of those tables for the lookup column value. As for this writing the multi table lookup features is in preview and is not available for configuration using the maker portal. To configure multi table relationships now you must use the Dataverse API.

Wrapping it up

Establishing the relationships between your tables in your data model is a critical step in designing your Dataverse data model. Relationships allow you to model real world interactions of the data. In order to avoid future problems, you must understand how the data is related and ensure the relationship type you choose doesn't limit the tracking of data interaction required by your app.

Relationship types and behaviors can be complex but with a little thought ahead of time you can find the right mix to ensure the table reacts the way your users would expect.

6

Data modeling

So far, we've been focused on capabilities of the Microsoft Dataverse for implementing a data model, in this module we look at the process of designing the model.

Having a solid data model for your app is probably one of the most important investments you make. The data model is like the foundation of a house, everything else is built on top of it. A bad data model can have long term impact on your app and the ongoing cost of maintenance as well as its ease of enhancement.

A data model goes through its own lifecycle as you conceive the initial version to enhancements down the road. The decisions you make on a clean slate at the beginning should be handled differently down the road as you have many apps and flows depending on its structure. It's important to not look at data modeling as just a onetime activity but something that evolves with the overall app. Your data model should be influenced over time by app user feedback, changes in the platform as well as changes in your requirements as business needs evolve.

While there are many opinions on how and where to start with data modeling, if you are migrating from an old system, simply copying what you had previously is probably the most dangerous starting point you can find. Not only will you inherit any shortcomings, it likely wasn't built with some of the platform considerations in mind. Most successful projects start with an open mind and take several aspects of their current requirements along with the platform capabilities in mind as they envision what the Dataverse data model for their app will look like.

Discovering data model needs

There are many possible places you can start the discovery of the data model and depending on the scale and complexity of your needs this can vary greatly. Simply put, there is no single right approach, however some combination of the following is appropriate for most scenarios.

Project Requirements

This is common on larger projects where there have been discovery workshops or other requirements gathering efforts that have collected from business users what is believed to be the requirements. Many times, these can include implementation suggestions and while valuable, should not be assumed to be the end of your discovery on data model needs. When presented with a set of formal requirements I like to conduct a triage pass through them making notes of things that might be good tables or key data fields that stand out. It is not uncommon to discover some of the security and data ownership issues that you will need to consider in your model.

User interviews/observations

Sitting down and watching a user do their work using the current environment can often highlight key data model and user experience aspects to consider. It's important to remember a key part of your project might be to come up with a new process that is completely different from today's business process. These sessions will allow you to glean key insights into things you might be able to do to automate or provide insights to improve their productivity. Many times, these result in data that needs to be collected or made available for the automation on insight evaluation.

I asked fellow MVP George Doubinski what was important here and he highlighted that you should try to get the following from these sessions:

- How the users work
- What are the most common data?
- What are the most common interactions?
- Issues and challenges
- Repeatable constructs
- Automation opportunities

Old Apps

While this can be a quick way to ramp up, it can also be a great way to convince you that the old app data model should be the starting point. I often like to review this after I've completed some rough data modeling design concepts using other sources if possible. Then deep diving on the old app looking for missed requirements. I also like to know what problems the old app had so if possible, we don't reintroduce them in the new app. Another key insight you can get from looking at the old apps data store is an idea of the volume of data.

Business Outcome Goals

Having a clear understanding of what the business is trying to accomplish is essential. This includes not only the process the app is automating, but the high-level management / sponsor goals.

Regulatory / Legal / Contractual requirements

Some data models have minimal influence by these where others have significant impact. In fact, in some scenarios this can require separate Dataverse environments to keep data isolated to comply. Pay particular attention to data that you might obtain from third parties, it's not uncommon that the contractual arrangement for use doesn't allow storing of the data. Of course, any sensitive information should also be evaluated. When appropriate, your data model might need to incorporate opt in/out as appropriate. Many modern laws (including GDPR) require end user disclosure of data you maintain about your customers. In those scenarios, the data you capture should always be consistent with what the company would be comfortable collecting and disclosing upon request. Many companies have people responsible for privacy and compliance that you should include in your efforts.

Reports and Analytics

In some cases, there may be existing reports or even visualizations used on the current process or the proposed app. These should be evaluated to determine if there is key data missing from your data model.

As important as existing reports and visualizations, what you plan to create for the new system is just as important. You can't produce reports or visualizations from data you didn't collect in the first place! This might include how you will bring operational data out of Dataverse into a data store that captures time series data.

AI and Insights

Just about everywhere you look these days apps say they use AI or provide insights. Simply put there is no magic that happens to produce these insights, they are data driven. In order to be able to have good AI models you must have the data signals to train the models. That starts as you build your data model by considering what data needs to be collected to support your current or future AI plans.

Have app, need a database

We can't overlook that in many cases you might be here because you built an app or a flow on Excel or SharePoint and realized you want to move to Dataverse. In these cases, you may be pretty far along on what you envisioned Dataverse to look like because you expected it to look just like what you built as version one. If you are short on time let's be honest this might be all you have time for and you just copy the design to Dataverse with as little change as possible. But when possible use your V1 as insight and go ahead and do a little more needs assessment. Often more is known, and things will evolve and it's a good time to make that happen.

Now and the future

One of the fine lines you will have to walk is how much you incorporate what might happen in the future. But, spending too much time designing a data model for the future will just result in tables being built that will never be used. That said not looking at what might change or things you know might happen can lead you to make data modeling decisions that won't scale with your needs. Generally, I like to suggest look 6-12 months out. Consider strong possible changes. Use those to influence your data model design but don't implement tables, fields and relationships for future enhancements until you are ready to build out things using them. This is a lot better than having to rip out a bunch of tables you never used.

Data model influencers

When designing your data model, in addition to your app requirements you should also take into consideration how Dataverse works. The following are things you should consider:

- **Self Service** – The Power Platform empowers users to build their own solutions. From Power BI to Power Apps and flow they can consume the data model you build. As you evaluate relationships and normalization of the data keep in mind each relationship can add complexity that a user needs to navigate to do their self-service tasks.

- **Security** – Security requirements can quickly increase complexity. Look to simplify whenever possible pushing back to achieve only true needs. Consider tools like sharing and field security to handle exceptions. Educate on value of collaboration and how you can use things like views to limit to assigned records. Understand the difference between security and a streamlined user experience. Security is to protect data, but you can design a good user experience and not need to "secure the data"; find out which is needed. Above all security by obscurity should be avoided because it really isn't security if you just hide it from the user.

- **Localization** – For apps that have this need, the data model should leverage things like choice lists over lookups to take advantage of the platform's built-in localization capabilities. In general, Power Apps model-driven apps have a lot of built-in support for localization, however some of your data model choices like lookups can defeat those capabilities and make it harder for you to localize your solution.

- **User Experience** – Power Apps model-driven apps are heavily influenced by the data model. Sometimes being a little less normalized can lead to a better user experience. The more you use things like manual many to many relationships and connections the more complex data entry is. Some of these experience impacts can be overcome by Power Apps canvas apps or Power Apps component framework controls. At the end of the day, users shouldn't care about the data model, as long as the data model cares about the users.

- **Accessibility** -Microsoft has prioritized accessibly and inclusive designs. As you design your customizations the burden falls to you to continue what was started. This should not be limited just to the notion of making your apps comply to the guidelines. This is more about inclusive design. You never know what problem you might solve. A good example is the "curb effect" you can read about it here
https://www.policylink.org/about-us/curb-cut-effect

Consider your roommates

When you are building a data model, I like to consider I might have roommates. In this context roommates are other data models for other apps that might share the same Dataverse deployment environment. Consider the following to be a good roommate:

- Don't rename CDM entities to be so specific they might not work for other solutions. For example, renaming Contact to People is fine, renaming Contact to Student is too narrow and not friendly to other solutions that might not have the same refined set of records.

- Use more qualified names of custom tables and choice lists to avoid collisions (e.g., Travel Categories instead of Categories).

- Don't include entity properties if not changing them. You can easily turn on/off auditing and other settings without intending to. Include entity metadata in your solution only when you are making changes to entity properties.

While you may be lucky and have the whole Dataverse to yourself, being a good roommate can ensure that even if that changes you will be in good shape.

What tools to use

Dataverse does not come with an official tool to design a data model. Dataverse tooling is focused on implementing the data model once designed. For designing you can use any tool you are comfortable with. Here are some suggestions that mostly focus on Entity and Relationships and not fields:

- Visio – This can help you visualize your data model.

- Any ERD tool – For traditional data modeling there are many entity relationship diagram (ERD) tools while not specifically for Dataverse they can be used. Keep in mind these often will have features that are not implementable by Dataverse so just use it to model the tables and relationships.

- Whiteboard – This is probably one of my favorite tools because they are everywhere in offices. While less formal, you can easily capture a picture of what you produce. In a pinch, you can also use any window or mirror to accomplish the same results.

- Excel – Not good for visualizing tables and relationships but great for capturing field details prior to creating in Dataverse.

Boil the ocean

Nothing paralyzes a team more than trying to solve a complex data model all at once. Generally speaking, almost every data model has some core parts that you can break up and solve as small pieces. Typically starting with the most obvious entity and adding the next few related tables is a great way to start. After identifying the core tables you can go back and add the relationship with indicators of 1:N or N:N next to it.

If you are part of a team, one thing you can try is challenging either a couple of small teams or multiple people to spend on hour or so trying to solve the data modeling problem. Then compare the different models. Oftentimes you will find that some combination of what the individual teams produce is the best answer.

Proof of concept

Getting a Dataverse environment to try your data model should be as easy as getting candy in a candy store. In a disposable environment, with a commitment to not use what you build as the real solution, quickly throw together a proof of concept of your core data model. Build a simple Power Apps model-driven app with the tables included. Use this to kick the tires of what you perceive is the perfect data model.

A key part of this is committing to it being throw-away so you don't have to worry about every single best practice as you throw together the data model and the app.

When a security model is complex, this is also a good time to include that as part of your proof of concept.

My Company Common Data Model

Take a page from Microsoft and create your own company common data model. As Power Platform takes off in your company many people will have the same data needs. Nothing says you can't package up your own CDM entities and offer it to teams as pre-built extension pack they can install and quickly get up on running using a common set of tables. Then their individual apps only worry about their own enhancements. This ensures a more consistent use of data across the company and it also makes app makers more productive.

Where to start

There is no single right way to get started with a data model, but I will offer some suggestions that might be helpful

- Start with what you know and are comfortable with
- Identify the most obvious tables
- Break complex topics into smaller models, you can put small data models together
- Don't worry too much about the fields unless they impact the overall design
- Worry about if it is a CDM entity or custom later, just draw a box with name at first
- Don't worry about duplication of tables in your first pass, if you draw Agent, Manager, VP and then later you can consolidate them all to users.
- Try not to shutdown crazy ideas people might have. Sometimes it's helpful to let them go work it out and come back and present it later
- Don't feel you have to detail the whole model in the first session – unless of course your project is due tomorrow.

Wrapping it up

Designing your data model is an investment you are making in the quality of the app you are building. Sure, it is tempting to jump right in and create your tables and fields, but instead take an appropriate amount of time and do a little bit of design. The key there is appropriate amount of time, which obviously will vary greatly across projects building on Dataverse.

7

Security modeling

When you build a business application you are storing data that must be protected. When you build a custom business application you start from zero and must design and implement your own security model. A key feature of the Microsoft Dataverse is a set of security features that can be used to craft a custom security model for you without having to do any custom code. Based on your requirements, you can choose which security features you want to enable/configure providing a lot of flexibility to handle a diverse set of security requirements.

As you work to define your data model you should also consider what your security model will look like as well. Many of the options you choose when you implement your data model also influence your security model choices. For example, when you choose table ownership of user/team vs. organization you choose how granular your security can be on that table.

In simple terms, users get permission to access data and services by having security roles assigned to them which grant privileges to perform operations and access data. An important concept to understand is that any grant of permission is cumulative across all grants to the user in an environment. There is no concept of taking away permissions, so be careful as you craft your security model to not over grant access because you can't reduce it later. In the rest of this chapter, we will dive deeper into how you define a security model for your application.

Building blocks

Dataverse provides multiple security building blocks that can be leveraged to build your security model. In this section we are going to look at each of the building blocks. The following are the key building blocks we will cover:

- Business Units
- Teams
- Table Ownership
- Security Roles
- Field Security
- Record Sharing
- Hierarchical Security

Business Units

Business units are useful for organizing users, teams and data. Think of them as a security boundary or container. By default, every Dataverse environment has a root business unit. This business unit is special because it can't be removed or re-parented as a child of another business units. In addition to the root business unit, you can create any number of child business units and they can too, have children thus creating a hierarchy. This hierarchy can be used to model groups of users and data that are related. The hierarchy can be used in security roles to grant privileges to not only the user's business units but children as well. Automation such as Power Automate can also use this hierarchy to filter triggering of automation.

While you could use this to directly model an organizational structure that often creates too many silos of users and data. For our purposes, let's assume that DaveCo has the following organizational structure:

```
              DaveCo
                 |
      ┌──────────┼──────────┐
    Sales              Customer
                       Support
      ┌──────────┼──────────┐
  Marketing          Manufacturing
```

As we work with DaveCo to understand how users work with their data, we learn that the data usage is more geared around a separation of Retail and Wholesale. We also learned that only managers work with data from both. If we look at how we might model our business units it probably would look more like the following example:

```
         DaveCo
            |
      ┌─────┴─────┐
    Retail    Wholesale
```

This will allow us to heavily use business unit level access for security roles which is very efficient.

Microsoft Dataverse users must be associated with a business unit. By default, this is the root business unit, but you can change this to be any in the business unit hierarchy. By putting a user in a business unit, you give security context. When a security role provides business unit level access it is given in the context of the user's assigned business unit.

In our example, we would place users in Retail and Wholesale based on their daily work. For managers who need to work daily with data from both, we could assign them to the root business unit DaveCo and then create security roles that give privileges that include child business unit access. As we will learn later in this chapter, teams (not to be confused with the Microsoft Teams app) can also be used to handle this type of requirement as well.

Business units support restructuring, allowing all but the root business unit to be moved around in the hierarchy. In our example, if DaveCo expanded into APAC, they could create a North American business unit and then place it above the existing Retail and Wholesale.

```
                        DaveCo
              ┌───────────┴───────────┐
            APAC                  North America
         ┌────┴────┐              ┌─────┴─────┐
     Wholesale   Retail         Retail     Wholesale
```

Moving business units in the hierarchy also moves its users, teams, and data records. This is helpful when you need to reorganize or expand. The only thing that changes is the privileges that include child business units will now reflect the new hierarchy.

Like users, data records that have entity ownership of user/team have a field that stores the business unit of user/team that owns the record. This is used to filter who can access the data and explains how Dataverse is able to efficiently resolve security done at the business unit level.

You should try to avoid moving users between business units as it requires re-assigning the user security roles as well as re-associating data records they own to the new business unit. Re-associating the records causes all records they own to have the owning business unit column updated and could cause performance impact if a large quantity of records are involved. This move could also remove access to data for users that remain in the old business unit because the data record is no longer associated with their business unit.

Because of the effort required to move users between business units, and to give flexibility design teams frequently create at least one child business unit instead of just putting everything in the root even for simple deployments. Take an example, where Mountain Ski deployed Dataverse, at the time they just used the root business unit because they didn't need child business units for their security model. If later, they merged with Ski Gear, Inc who builds ski gear and wanted to migrate Ski Gear, Inc's data into the same Dataverse environment it would be somewhat painful to reorganize business units. If they had planned ahead and even though they didn't need child business units they create one child anyway it would make it easier to handle the merger. So their initial setup would look something like the following:

```
        Mountain
          Ski
            |
   Mountain |
     Ski ───┘
```

Now with this structure in place, when they later merged with Ski Gear, Inc they could easily restructure to include Ski Gear, Inc. The following shows what it looks like after the merger:

```
              Mountain
                Ski
                 |
        ┌────────┴────────┐
    Mountain           Ski Gear,
      Ski                Inc
```

Using this approach, they would not have to move the existing users and simply add the new business units.

As you consider your business unit structure always keep them to the minimum you need for your security model to ensure best performance while honoring the data access requirements. If you simply need segmentation of users or other groupings for offices and departments, consider using teams instead.

Teams

Teams are groups of users. Each team is owned by a single business unit. We will see how this ownership impacts security role configuration later. Each business unit has a default team automatically created when the business unit is created. This default team tracks all the users that are associated with that business unit automatically and does not allow you to manually add or delete of users. Additionally, you can create your own custom teams and have complete control over the membership. In fact, teams that you create can contain users from different business units allowing you to solve some cross business unit collaboration security challenges.

Teams can have security roles associated with them to convey permissions to the team members for accessing data and services. These permissions are granted in the context of the business unit that owns the team making it a powerful way to give users from other business units access without moving them into the team's business unit.

There are different types of teams, each having different features that can help you build a complete security model. The following are the different types:

- **Owner** – This is the original team type and allows the team to be an owner of records.

- **Access** – This type of team cannot own records but can be used to gain access by sharing a record with the team. Using an access team template this process can be automated including creating of the team and adding the members on the fly and granting them access by sharing the record with the team. This is helpful for record scenarios where you have a dynamic team that works on each record that you need to build and manage.

- **Group** - Teams that are configured with groups connect to either an Azure Active Directory security group or an Office 365 group. The membership of these teams is managed by their associated Azure/Office 365 group. These groups can be created automatically for you when you share an app in the portal with and Azure group. Like access groups these groups can also not own records. This is the best approach for giving users access to an app and data in one operation and makes it easy for admins to administer your security model.

It is not uncommon for a security model to use all three different types of teams to handle specific scenarios within the model. Teams are generally a lighter weight approach than business units for managing groups of users and records.

Table Ownership

We covered this in the table chapter however table ownership also impacts your security model and how security role privileges can be set as well. Tables can be either organization or user/team owned. Organization owned allow limited configuration of the access levels compared to user/team owned. You should only use organization owned when you don't need granular security control now or in the future. Table ownership can only be set at creation so it's important to get it right. When in doubt use user/team ownership.

Security Roles

Security roles are used to determine what data and operations a user can access or perform. Each role is a set of privileges, each having an access level configured. The privilege is the what e.g. read the contact table and the access level is what data you can access. For tables that are organization owned access level is all or none. For tables that can be user/team owned the following are the access levels available:

- **None** – The default for new privileges and grants no additional access.

- **User** – When the user owns the record, they have this privilege. For example, if the user had read contact privilege set to user and they owned a contact record they would be able to read it, but they would not be able to read records owned by other users.

- **Business Unit** - This gives the user the privilege to access when the record is owned by a user or team in their associated business unit. This is a common setting to allow collaboration among a department or division of people. For example, the salesperson can see all accounts in the same business unit.

- **Parent:Child Business Units** – This gives the user the privilege to access when the record is owned by a user team in the associated business unit or its child business units. This is commonly used to give managers access to the whole organization or a part of the organization that has been broken up and managed by business units.

- **Organization** - This gives the privilege of access regardless of who owns the record. This is the broadest form of access that you can grant. Care should be taken to not grant this access when not required because there is no way to reduce the access once organization level access is granted without changing the user's security roles or editing the role itself.

When you are editing a security role these are set by clicking on the circle for each of the privileges to control the access level. The following are what the visual indicator looks like for each level:

| None Selected | User | Business Unit | Parent: Child Business Units | Organization |

To configure a security role, you set the access level for each privilege, and for each table as needed.

Security Role: New Security Role

Entity	Create	Read	Write	Delete	Append	Append To	Assign	Share
Account	○	○	○	○	○	○	○	○
ACIViewMapper	○	○	○	○				
Action Card	○	○	○	○	○	○	○	
Action Card User Settings	○	○	○	○				○
Activity	○	○	○	○	○	○	○	○
Advanced Similarity Rule	○	○	○	○	○	○		
Announcement	○	○	○	○		○		
Application File	○	○	○	○				
Azure Service Connection	○	○	○	○	○	○		
Category	○	○	○	○	○	○	○	○
Connection	○	○	○	○	○	○	○	○
Connection Role	○	○	○	○	○	○		
Contact	○	○	○	○	○	○	○	○

Tip: To speed up setting all privilege values for a table you can click on the table name and it will cycle through all the access levels for that table. You can also do the same by clicking on a privilege and it will change the values for all tables.

Each table has eight privileges that determine what a user can do on each row. Create, Read, Write and Delete are just what they say they are. Share allows the user to give access to the row to another user. Append is required to allow rows from this table to be associated to another table. For example, an email activity can be attached to a contact table row if the user has Append rights on the email activity table. Append To is required to allow associating another table row with the current row. Using the same example Append to would be required on the contact table to allow associating the email activity. Most commonly these privileges are both allowed on a role but can be turned off or limited to have finer control of what records can be associated or disassociated by the user.

One or more security roles can be associated with a user or team to establish the permissions that they have. When a user or team has multiple security roles assigned, their access level is the composite of all security roles combined. It is important to understand that when a user or team has multiple it is the greatest access provided that prevails if one role has less and another has more. There is no way to configure a security role to reduce the permissions of what another role already provides the user. For this reason, care should be taken when assigning security roles did not over grant privileges.

Microsoft Dataverse as well as the applications you install may come with prebuilt security rules. A good practice is to copy the roles that you want and tailor them as needed for your solution. Just as it's important to add anything that is unique to your solution it is also important to reduce the privileges granted for things your solution does not use. The advantage of copying the rolls is two part. First, some security roles have hidden privileges that you cannot add or set through the editor and must be copied to retain them. Second, your users will only have the permissions that you give them, and they will not have surprise permissions granted. Be aware that if Microsoft or the app publisher later changes the original security role it won't change your copy you have to manually make that change.

For users to access any custom tables you created you must create a security role that has privileges configured for that table. There are different approaches you can take. For example, some create a base security role that all users have and then specialization roles for each functional role like sales or service.   A user in the system is then assigned the base role plus the functional role giving them the combined permissions. Another approach is to copy an existing role and tailor it for each functional role. With this approach your base settings are duplicated on each functional role, however, you only have one role to assign to users/teams instead of two.

One setting on the security role you should pay attention to if you are using security roles with teams is the When role is assigned to a team setting. When set to Team privileges only if a user doesn't have another role giving them user privileges, they can only create records that are owned by the team. When set to the default, Direct user it's like the privileges were directly assigned to the user similar to when a security role is directly assigned to a user instead of a team. This means your security model can fully use teams to assign all privileges to users and not have to rely on individual user assignment. This makes administration easier.

When role is assigned to a team
Team member gets all team privileges by default.
Team members can inherit team privileges directly based on access level. Learn More

Member's privilege inheritance: Direct User (Basic) access level and ▼
- Team privileges only
- Direct User (Basic) access level and Team privileges

Field Security

Security roles focus on if a user can access or perform an operation on a row/record of data. Field security allows you to protect individual columns of data. Field level security is configured on a column-by-column basis. Most system fields that contain personal identifiable information can be enabled for field level security. Any custom column you create can also be enabled.

Field level security can be used to determine if the user can create, update, or read that column's data. This can be used to handle a number of scenarios such as when a user needs to be able to update or modify the data but not be able to read the existing data or for example when the user does not have permission to modify the data but does have permission to be able to read the data.

Once enabled for a column, users are no longer able to access the data until a field security profile is created and associated with a user or team. The field level security profile identifies for each secured column the permission to create, update, or read the data. For example, if you had a discount amount you might have a field security profile for managers that allowed create, update, and reading the discount amount and another one for salespeople that only allowed reading it.

While it might be tempting to enable this feature for all custom columns care should be taken to only enable it where necessary. Field security adds additional overhead to operations to check to see if the user has the ability to perform the requested action.

Record Sharing

Record sharing allows you to establish permissions for a user or team to have access to just a single record or row. Record sharing is intended to handle exceptions in your security model.

The reason this is for exceptions is because the performance can be greatly impacted the more record sharing that is completed in an environment. Each share creates a record in a principal object access table that has to be evaluated anytime the system is going to grant access to the record. When you do have to use record sharing, share with a team instead of individual users if possible. This creates only one record in the principal object access table to track all the users in the team instead of one for each user.

In order for a record to be shared with a user or a team that user or team must have at least user level of the privilege that you are sharing. When considering using sharing you should also evaluate if using an owning or access team might be a better alternative.

If you find your users manually sharing frequently you might review to see if using access team templates might be more efficient. For example, in a real estate solution you have a Deal table, you might setup a deal team access template giving access to the deal table. Then by adding a sub-grid on the deal table form you can easily allow adding deal team members who will be granted access to the deal record without having to do the manual record sharing.

Hierarchical Security

Hierarchical security can help with scenarios where a user needs to access records for the hierarchy of other users they manage or work with. Microsoft Dataverse supports manager and position hierarchical access. Manager hierarchical access uses the manager column on the user record to determine access. Position hierarchical access uses a custom position like sales manager or customer service manager to build the hierarchy and grant access.

When configured hierarchical access grants users at the higher level of the hierarchy access to lower levels. For one level below, access is the same as the managed user. Access for those greater than one level below is read-only. This includes records directly owned or owned by a team the user is a member of and also records shared.

Designing a security model

The security model should be designed during the first part of the project alongside of the data model and user experience. Project teams that wait till the end risk data model changes to accommodate for security requirements. Designing involves using all the building blocks together to address the security requirements identified. The design should take in to consideration all layers of the application. The following are some key principles that should be considered during the design:

- Simple is good.
- Challenge complex requirements and weigh the real risks.
- Obscuring data from viewing is not data security. E.g., removing a field from a form, view or app screen is not securing it.
- Pushing security as low in the app layers ensures all apps and automation built follow it. E.g., using Dataverse field security is better than app logic doing the same thing.
- Using automation or code with elevated permissions can avoid direct assignment of broad permissions to users.
- Avoid data silos and encourage collaboration when possible.
- Consider impact to other existing or future apps that might be in same environment.
- When in doubt use user/team table ownership instead of organization.
- The design must be manageable with provided resources.
- Consider auditing functionality to allow less restrictive access.
- Is there real impact if other users read this data? Allowing more liberal read access can reduce a lot of usability and performance issues.
- Consider multiple smaller apps that reduce user's clutter if restricting access is actually a convenience request.

Your job is to design a security model that protects sensitive data and at the same time encourages collaboration and allows the business process to happen as needed without unnecessary friction. If you design something overly complex and unmanageable it won't be long before it becomes subverted by over granting of permissions to keep the business running. An important way to do that is by fully understanding the real security model requirements by asking questions and clarifications. It's also important to challenge things that lead to complexity and try to drive towards simplification.

The first step in security model design is understanding the groups of users that will be using the solution you are architecting. It's important to understand what data they will use and how that data is shared among the groups of users. You should be clear if any requests for isolation of data is to simplify the user's task and where it is a requirement to secure the data due to sensitivity. Isolation for simplicity should consider if views or tailored forms, or even a tailored app would provide a better solution.

As you first review the requirements that are used to build the app or solution you should be looking for things that could be called out as security requirements and tagging them or setting them aside for review. As soon as possible if you identify a requirement that is not capable of being implemented on the platform you should work to try to negotiate it to something that is implementable. As you review requirements you should identify them as either standard or exception. To understand that you must ask questions that clarify how often that particular situation occurs so you can properly assess the requirement.

As the project progresses reevaluate the security model choices you have made especially the more complex ones. It is common that as the project progresses you understand more about the business problem trying to be solved and might be able to make more appropriate suggestions to simplify what was originally envisioned as a complex security model. Testing the system as users of the various roles is vital, make sure that is part of the test plan.

Wrapping it up

Taking time to build your security model is essential. Like a data model, the security model is part of your solution's foundation that you build apps and automation on top of. A poor security model can lead to lack of user adoption and performance issues. Invest early in your project to ensure you build a good security model.

Printed in Great Britain
by Amazon